THE
QUALIFICATION STRUGGLE

BRAM VAN OIRSCHOT

Author: Bram van Oirschot

The information in this book is for general guidance only. The author and publisher make no representations or warranties of any kind, express or implied, about the completeness, accuracy, reliability, suitability, or availability of the information in this book for any purpose. Any reliance you place on such information is therefore strictly at your own risk.

© Bram van Oirschot 2023

All rights reserved. No part of this book may be reproduced or transmitted in any form or by any means, electronic or mechanical, including photocopying, recording, or by any information storage and retrieval system, without permission in writing from the author.

ISBN: 9798850373658 (paperback)

Imprint: Independently published

First printed edition: August 2023

Published by Bram van Oirschot

Diessen, The Netherlands

Preface

My time is precious, as is yours.

Like you, I hate spending time on things that do not take me further. I dedicate my life to adding value to sales professionals and clients. At the same time, I want the people around me to work on the projects they like.

Like you, I have been trying to understand why qualification is so difficult. I tried to make a qualification checklist in Excel, but it got me nowhere. I have attempted traditional qualification frameworks but subsequently found them inappropriate and redundant.

Further, like you, I get inspired from working on opportunities and projects that benefit from my team's competencies. A project that fits perfectly gives people the enthusiasm to excel.

For two decades, my teams and I have studied the qualification process. As a result, we have learned many valuable lessons and continue to perfect our strategy. Many of the lessons learned are presented to you in this book.

You will learn why traditional frameworks simply do not work. These frameworks are designed for a status quo. They do not promote growth and, instead, put any entrepreneurial spirit you once had, to sleep.

Instead, many factors play a significant role in the qualification process. I have found them and will share them with you today.

After reading this book, you will be more confident when qualifying opportunities. In addition, you will soon be rewarded with a healthy project pipeline supporting the growth you envision and deserve. It is not as difficult as you think. However, it would be best if you had someone to guide you.

So, why did I write this book?

This book was my entrance into the consultancy world. I would give it away for free to get into contact with entrepreneurs. I selected this topic because it naturally grabs the attention of business owners. They feel The Qualification Struggle every day. They worry about not having enough work for their entire company. Or, they are wasting valuable personal and family time on ghost opportunities.

This book taps right into the pain of the readers. The idea was that the reader would call me straight after reading this book. Then, I would guide business owners in a direction that would do justice to their companies' competencies and promote the growth path they were dreaming of.

My career, however, took a different path. I became a business owner myself. As a result, I feel the Qualification Struggle myself every day.

Nevertheless, this book contains valuable content that will benefit others like me. It is no longer a lead generation book, so you must spend a couple of bucks to enjoy my lessons. However, you will save twenty years studying the topic and become more successful.

Contents

Preface — iii

Introduction — 1
Who Should Read This Book?..7
My Promise..9

Why Qualification — 13
1.1 Corporate Resources..18
1.2 The Objective...23

Client Pressures — 27
2.1 Qualifying Dream Clients..29
2.2 Qualifying Future A Clients..35
2.3 Qualification for Urgency...41
2.4 Standard Qualification Frameworks....................................47
2.5 Summary...53

Internal Pressures — 57
3.1 The Influence of Appetite...59
3.2 Organizational Ambition..66
3.3 Project Execution Constraints..73
3.4 Project Potential 's Impact..80
3.5 Summary...87

Personal Pressures — 91

4.1 Personal Timing 95
4.2 Personal Fear 102
4.3 Personal Excitement 109
4.4 New-Colleagues 115
4.5 Summary 122

Tender Pressures — 125

5.1 Tender Process 127
5.2 Supply Chain Pressures 134
5.3 Specs Pressures 140
5.4 Project Fit 147
5.5 Summary 151

Implementation — 155

6.1 Building Blocks 158
6.2 My Unique Qualification Process 160
6.3 Involve Your Client 167
6.4 Summary 174

Conclusion – Next Steps — 177

About the Author — 180

Introduction

I had just bought my first house together with my girlfriend, whom I married a few years later. I had traveled the world for the past four years selling lifting services to operators of offshore platforms and owners of refineries. A lot of my time was spent on planes between continents. Selling was not my dream job, and I was certainly not the average salesperson.

I was spending all my time planning my trips, meeting clients, and working to provide the best possible solutions to their challenges. I was getting myself into as many commercial battles as I could handle. It seemed like my life was all about selling, but in my mind, I knew it was an investment.

I was unsure about the goal I had in life. It certainly was not going to be chasing contracts all my life. What I was sure of was that the selling experiences would be a solid foundation for my future career.

I was one of those guys always on the move. I hate to waste time waiting or chasing the wrong opportunities. I always had the feeling that I was wasting my time and using my valuable free time.

As much as I enjoyed grinding my way through the oceans of opportunities, I hated the waiting. I was upset when I traveled halfway around the world to find out a meeting was canceled. Although it only resulted in a gap in my agenda of a few hours, it made me nervous. I started to call my network if they were up for a cup of coffee. I did a lot to prevent wasted time.

I was raised by entrepreneurial parents. They had more than enough time for me, but they planted a belief that time is of the essence, always. This belief serves me well most of the time. It has provided me with a nose for efficiency.

In my mid-thirties I realized more and more that time is the most precious gift of life. You can spend time on the things you like. You can trade your time to create freedom. I came to realize that I could not only sell my time but that others were also ready to invest in my goals.

Time is a finite resource. You cannot get the seconds back that have just passed. You cannot use the time of others twice. It is our responsibility to make efficient use of the time we have.

After spending a decade on the road, I started to understand how to use my time more effectively. We lost a fair number of opportunities after submitting a quotation. I realized that the key to success was in the qualification process. And that, I had no idea how to improve.

During that period, I became more and more frustrated by the commercial process. It felt like I was losing my grip on commercial situations.

In May 2013, this came to a climax. I had a full sales pipeline and was about to close a vast number of contracts. But, it seemed like life was about to teach me an important lesson. A lesson in failure.

Four major contracts should have been signed by the end of the month. In a typical month, I would only have one or two of these contracts, but in spring 2013, four commercial processes were about to end. I was very optimistic about my chances on at least three of them but guessed that I would also close the fourth.

The first project was a skidding project in Bangladesh for a Singaporean EPC contractor. I had worked with the company before, and they indicated that we were in the front seat of winning the contract. When I rang them on the day of my birthday, they told me that they had awarded the contract to an Asian competitor. What had happened? How could they do this to me? I helped them substantially in the previous project and provided them with all the support during this tender.

On the same day, I got a message from a client in Australia. They had canceled a project on which I worked for a few months in 2012. It was postponed a couple of times, but now the operator had the funds available to start the project. Nevertheless, the project took a different turn. I asked myself if I should celebrate my birthday. It was not really my lucky day.

One week later I won a small job in my home country, the Netherlands. I hoped that this would be a prerequisite for my chances of getting the other two profitable projects.

This was not the case. The third project was one that was out of our normal scope of supply. The scope of work was to remove a small facility just offshore of Malaysia. My offer included a partner, which involved some third-party costs. Attached to these third-party costs was a set of equipment that had a large day rate. Delays would immediately jeopardize the project. The risk was quite high, but I thought the margins would compensate. Just before we had to submit the Best and Final Offer, my management decided to decline the opportunity and withdrew from the tender process. I could have estimated this course of action way before but was naive.

The fourth project was a small lifting job in Angola on one of the Floating Production Storage and Offloading (FPSO) units. We lost the job to a regular competitor in a fair battle of pricing.

How could these four events happen in one month? What was life about to teach me? Was it trying to tell me that I should not try to win contracts in May, or was there something more rational I could do to improve my chances?

I became more convinced that the solution could be found in the qualification process. During the summer holiday, I could not get my head around the process and decided to educate myself. I did not want to waste any more time on projects. Not my time, not the time of my colleagues, and not the time of partners. It had to stop.

I gathered books, turned YouTube into my best friend, and listened to podcasts. I soon dived into the world of traditional qualification methods. The grassroots of qualification lie in the 1950s when the BANT methodology was developed by IBM to teach their new salespeople how to sell. It is still the most widely used framework.

More modern theories promised better and more sophisticated results. Dick Dunkel introduced MEDDIC in the early days of his career. He understood the complexity of larger decision-making units. Further criteria were added in the MEDDPICC method, which takes the tender specs and the competition into account.

My search continued along the paths of PMAR, FAINT, GPCTBA/C&I, CHAMP, and ANUM; all exotic abbreviations promising different solutions for my challenge. I started to use a few of these systems and enjoyed the initial successes.

The systematic approach to new opportunities was welcomed by my managers. They felt that I was going to make more rational decisions on the use of their valuable resources. They believed that this was the solution for developing a laser-sharp sales machine: target only opportunities that would fit the core competencies of the company, at the right time and on the right terms.

Initially, I felt satisfied with the results. I felt recognized by my peers and by my manager. It was only a matter of time before harvesting the economic fruits of my new system. I believed the traditional qualification frameworks were the holy grail to realize a streamlined and effective sales pipeline. I used different systems for a year and experienced some successes.

I kept using these frameworks for another few months with limited results. I still was not fully satisfied. My colleagues kept pulling me into qualification meetings and they pressured me with factors that were not part of the traditional frameworks. They showed me some flaws in the system by presenting objections to most opportunities. Sometimes it was a special condition in the contract, sometimes it was the supply chain that was causing concerns.

On the other hand, I felt held back by the same frameworks. I felt that they were trying to knock down my entrepreneurial spirit. Sometimes, opportunities just felt right. I could not pinpoint what made the difference. It was just a feeling that I had about some opportunities. I felt that the complex nature of international B2B service sales cannot be completely boxed into fixed categories. There should always be room to be exempt from rigid qualification systems.

I re-visited all the opportunities that I declined over the previous 18 months. I studied the criteria on which tenders were disqualified and concluded that there were some really nice opportunities left on the table.

When staring down at the list of declined opportunities, my commercial heart broke. We could have done so much more. We could have entered new markets, penetrated new accounts, and we could have had so much more fun with these nice challenges. We were hiding behind a qualification wall and neglected our growth ambitions. The appetite for new projects that I was feeling two years ago, was gone.

By adopting the systematic qualification approach, we lost a lot, we lost the excitement of a new challenge, the risky challenge, and the feeling of working on the unknown. I was sure this was not the way to become rich either.

I started gathering data on all our opportunities. I also involved sister companies and started to interview salespeople in the industry. And, within three years, I had all the data I needed to make the qualification process complete.

I noticed that a lot of criteria were affecting the qualification process. I came to realize that the traditional qualification frameworks were a good tool for salespeople to structure their sales conversations, but less useful to qualify opportunities. The exotic abbreviations help salespeople to get the maximum of every sales situation, but should not be used to qualify complex opportunities.

I gathered all the concepts and turned them into a unique toolset that can make you rich. The toolset will provide guidance to create your unique qualification process. It will take short-term and mid-term organizational goals into account and allow you to become rich by focusing on the right opportunities.

Selling is the art of disqualification. When you are becoming good at what you do, opportunities will flow your way. It is disqualification that makes you rich, by accepting only the opportunities that bring you closer to your goals.

Since 2018, I have been using the extended qualification criteria in my own practice. I use it to fill my pipeline with healthy projects. Some opportunities bring in a lot of fun and excitement, others add to business continuity and growth. There should always be a mix of different kinds of opportunities, so your organization stays motivated and fosters a healthy appetite for growth.

I have been teaching the method to others in our industry on a global scale. The things that I will teach you in this book have transitioned me from a salesperson who chases with all his energy, to a salesperson who uses the scarce resource of time to become rich.

INTRODUCTION

Who Should Read This Book?

This book is written for people who are feeling confused and exhausted by the qualification process. The people who feel that their teams are chasing the wrong opportunities. The people who feel too many resources are wasted on opportunities that do not bring in value.

We often get asked by various company's management to educate their sales teams. Those companies do not want to kill the entrepreneurial spirit of their salespeople but want to provide them with the right toolset to remain focused on the opportunities that bring value to the company objectives.

This book is for managers of sales teams to arm them with the tools to get their challenging projects qualified. These managers understand that traditional qualification frameworks are adequate to educate their teams on how to sell. But, they also understand that these systems are not designed to get the go-ahead on the pearls presented by prospects.

Lastly, the experienced salesperson will feel recognized by the contents of the book. It will be a relief that there is more to sales than BANT, MEDDIC, or one of those other frameworks that they were made to adopt. It is those salespeople who hate to fill the template with wishy-washy reasons to qualify opportunities. They feel that they need more tools to get the best opportunities across the qualification bar.

In short, this book is for people who want to become rich by disqualification.

INTRODUCTION

My Promise

You are already at the second stage of your journey. You are reading this book because you feel there is more to learn about disqualification. You hope to find the tools needed to get to the next step in your career. You feel that there is a lot to gain when qualifying opportunities.

You are right. Disqualification makes you rich!!

I devoted a big part of my career to this process that lies in front of you. I want you to become successful and I promise you that I will be on your side during your journey. I get inspired by the success of others. Your success is my professional happiness.

When you are finished reading this book, you can create your own unique qualification process. It requires you to do some hard work.

I am here to provide you with the tools, but you need to implement them into your daily routines. This requires discipline and dedication. It also requires your colleagues to understand the system.

I am here to guide you even after completing this book. My team and I have developed all kinds of tools to keep you going on the path to perfection. These tools are available online.

Besides that, we are available to be consulted directly to answer the questions you have. Reach out to me and my team with any questions. We can get you on one of our programs or provide you with personal consults.

We have a lot to share and are here to help you along the path to commercial success.

Why Qualification

What is the worst thing that has happened to you in sales? Was it the biggest deal of your life that you lost to a competitor? Was it the contract that was canceled just after you thought you crossed the finish line?

Think hard …

You have fought so many sales battles. The ones that you remember are the ones where you were not alone. You have battled alongside your colleagues and probably alongside your clients. You were out on the front line and were supported by the troops behind you. If you won the battle, you won together. If you did not win, you lost together.

Losing a fair battle is not the worst. At least not in sales.

Not participating in your selected battle is the worst.

You have put tremendous hours to get to a point where you received a request from a new prospect, or from within a new industry, to find out that your troops are not supporting you. Or worse, you used internal and external resources to create the perfect offer, but were overruled and you had to call back on submission.

Those experiences get under my skin.

I do not feel supported by the traditional qualification frameworks. It seems that they have been designed by engineers to make sure their workload is manageable. Traditional qualification frameworks kill entrepreneurship and creativity.

I believe in a flexible world where exceptions to the status quo let us grow, and always allow for exceptions to guidelines. In today's world, change happens fast. Sometimes, you have to jump on a train without knowing where it will take you. When it feels good, embark.

It is the responsibility of sales to move the boundaries of the organization. It is sales that should fuel change to grow the business. It is our responsibility to bring in a steady flow of business, including a healthy pipeline of new kinds of business.

A Story

Throughout this book, you will find many stories from my own experience or from the people I coached. You will easily relate to them because they are not unique. They are probably the kinds of stories that you experience daily.

You will recognize the emotional rollercoaster I embarked on a few years ago. This is a true story that forms the foundation for this book.

The company I was working for was transitioning from an engineering company to a full-service contractor. They were lucky to get a first contract that they took over from a client that went bankrupt. This project provided them with the first line on their track record and with some very useful equipment. In this project, a living quarter module was installed on an offshore platform.

With this reference in hand, I started exploring the market for similar opportunities. I was hired to give the transformation of the company a commercial boost, so the pressure was on me. After months of researching and prospecting, a real opportunity was presented to me by a manufacturer of living quarters. The prospect took the installation of the module into their scope of work, which was not part of their usual service portfolio. They found a savior in my company.

We accepted this opportunity. The technical challenge was obvious, but the devil was in the details. The project took place in Libya with the transport from Rotterdam to Libya quoted lumpsum as well, and all parties were relatively inexperienced in this kind of project.

We qualified the opportunity based on an entrepreneurial spirit. Most would say it was a naive decision. We justified it by the new market potential, the excitement of the project, that the project would be 'next level' in the direction we wanted to develop, and we could use the equipment we already had in place. We took the risks for granted.

When qualifying, we felt comfortable having an initial engineering phase. We had the feeling that we could always pull back during this phase.

The project took off at a good pace. The engineering went well and our engineers identified a working technical solution. I traveled to Libya on multiple occasions because our initial Dutch client wanted to get rid of their transport and installation responsibility. I worked on the contract together with the client in Libya.

During these trips, I noticed the challenging local environment. It was a strange time in Libya. The Gaddafi regime was about to fall and several groups were fighting for power. I remember one meeting at the client's office when we heard a loud noise. The client said that a new vessel was welcomed by a canon in the harbor. I pretended I believed it and we continued the discussion on the project.

We were getting into the project. We noticed that we had implicitly accepted the project already. We skipped parts of the qualification process. We initially qualified for the engineering scope, but we just went on into the project without proper qualification.

I was very motivated to win this deal. This would be a record project for me. It would provide me with a lot of personal satisfaction, and it would really secure my position within the company. All of these personal ambitions influenced the qualification process significantly.

How did the Project End?

The exemplary opportunity would for sure pass the traditional qualification frameworks, like BANT or MEDDIC. We addressed the right needs, understood the decision-making unit, identified the availability of budget, and we could meet the required timeline. All signs were green.

But we should have realized all the potential risks that were involved. The project took place in Libya, which was going through a rough period. The extent of the project was way beyond what we had ever done before, and the client had not ever performed such a challenging exercise. We could be faced with significant penalties if we did not meet the deadline. This is often the reason why traditional qualification methods fall short in complex selling environments like in international contracting.

When selling projects, we accept a certain level of risk. There is often a strong correlation between the level of risk and the potential gains (or losses). The more risk in the project, the greater the potential for gains, and the stakes are higher as well. This is the result of the scarcity of contractors willing to take the risk. Scarcity drives the price up because margins have to be incorporated in setting the price.

If we had thought about the risk versus reward ratio and run it past BANT, MEDDIC, or any other method, chances are we would have accepted if the appetite for gains was great enough. Therefore, appetite is one of the factors described in this book.

If we were to make a long-term decision, it would include the potential of the client. If we qualify opportunities for dream clients, or from top prospects in new markets, we would be more likely to qualify opportunities like the example I've given above.

All these factors will be addressed in this book, but they only matter if they are used in a systematic way. There should be a system in place, a kind of stop-and-go system. If you pass one step of qualification, you continue to the next step. At every step, you might consider the opportunity qualified. But, do not disqualify the opportunity based on just one stop. Always consider other factors.

Remember, the worst thing that you can do is not adopt a qualification process.

The second worst thing is to accept all opportunities. It is your responsibility to make effective use of resources.

1.1 Corporate Resources

Salespeople, like most humans, are driven by instincts. We want to say 'yes' to every opportunity, close the sale, and add value. However, unlike animals, we can reason beyond our primary instincts. We have to use this skill in the commercial process. It helps us to provide more value to the right project without wasting too much energy.

We have an obligation to look beyond our own resources. The resources we tap into are scarce as well. The time of your colleagues is limited. The resources of those bright minds should be directed where they can add the most value. If there are other people outside your organization more suitable to meet the demands of your client, you have an obligation to point your client in the right (most effective) direction. Market mechanisms will do the rest.

The qualification process should help us approach the right projects and focus on suitable opportunities. It is all about using resources wisely.

Types of Resources

In the qualification process, two types of resources are relevant in two different project phases. We distinguish internal and external resources in the tender phase and in the execution phase.

The internal resources are available from within your company and use the time, skills, and competencies of yourself and of your colleagues.

External resources are available outside your organization. They are the same type of resources as internal, but they need to be acquired from within partner or subcontractor organizations.

In the qualification process, we identify tangible resources as something that everyone can buy. Tangible resources are internal or external depending on who is investing and who turns these tangible resources into added value. If you buy a prototype to support your tender, it becomes your internal resource. If your partner or subcontractor makes the prototype available, we consider it an external resource.

Resources are required in the tender process and in the execution process. All the resources to create the bid are part of the tender process. Most often, they are not paid for or only partially reimbursed. The tender resources are part of the overhead of the company. They are used to create business for the rest of the organization.

The resources required to execute the project are those that add value to the client and for which the client is paying directly. The value of these resources is what determines the net cost of the project. In the construction industry, this phase is called the construction phase. In other industries, this phase might be called the delivery phase, operational phase, or project phase.

Different types of resources add specific dynamics to the project. Internal resources during the tender phase are used to create perceived value together with external resources. Both internal and external resources are aligned to win the contract. In the execution phase, the external resources will be added as subcontractors into the final delivery, or your resources will be added to the external service as a semi-finished product.

Abundance of Resources

Organizations are set up in a way that all available resources are used. Besides realizing revenue targets, there is the need to maximize the utilization factor. Why do we strive for a 100% utilization factor?

We use it as an excuse for not realizing other KPIs. If we are not spending all the capacity we can, and we are not making the targets, we feel that we are doing a bad job. We feel that we have done everything in our power if we used all the resources available to us.

Another reason why we try to hit 100% utilization every time is to secure the resources for the future. If we outperform our targets with less than the maximum resources available, we might have fewer resources in the future. If our sales team sells too much for the company to handle, the size of our sales team will be questioned. If we have to decrease the size, we might not hit our numbers in the next period.

It would serve us well if we could remove the link between utilization factors and performance targets. We should use the surplus of capacity (if any) to make our processes more efficient, so fewer resources are required to perform the same task in the future. The improved processes will prepare us for future challenges and provide a foundation for further growth.

In the qualification process, a surplus of tender resources can result in accepting less suitable opportunities. Tender teams will feel the need to spend all of their resources to secure these resources for the future. This trend will not add value to us in the future. Of course, internal capacity plays a role in the qualification process, but it should be used wisely.

A temporary excess of tender capacity should be used to optimize business processes. If the rest of the organization is full for a certain period, the tender capacity can be used to automate parts of the sales process, to create service portfolios that clients of the future might want, or to support other departments in fulfilling their tasks. We should make our teams more flexible and stimulate interdepartmental cooperation. This will not only be good for the company, it will also benefit the qualification process. It will result in less waste of resources.

Time is of the essence

Time is the most important factor in the qualification process. Other resources can be obtained without personal sacrifices. Time is what people have a shortage of. We want to spend our time performing tasks that make the best use of our time. If we have to spend time filling in forms, we feel our time is undersold. If we have to spend family time finishing the bid within a deadline, we consider it an investment.

If we lose opportunities, the lost time is what causes us the most headaches. If we need to ask people around us, including external parties, to invest time in our opportunities, we feel that their main concern is the amount of time they need to invest and cannot spend on other tasks.

If we are pushing the limits of capacity, it is the time factor that will cause the most problems in the long run. If we over-utilize time it will result in burnouts and mistakes. It will have personal consequences.

The younger generation appreciate their work, but consider it work. It is not the only thing that counts in their lives. They want to live a life in which they have time to do fun things or to make the world a better place. They are looking for a purpose more than looking to win the next project at their personal expense.

It is the factor of time that is relevant. We need to use our time wisely to add the most value to the world. We should disqualify less fitting opportunities to have a rich life: a life full of fulfillment.

1.2 The Objective

The objective of the qualification process and of this book is to become rich. When I started my career, I focused on getting rich on experiences. By traveling the world and getting myself into an overwhelming number of sales situations. Those experiences made me the sales pro I consider myself to be today. I have spent a lot of my time creating the perfect selling system with a clear goal in mind. I wanted to become the best salesperson in industrial sales.

I qualified opportunities based on the level of excitement it offered me. The stranger the opportunity, the more I liked it. The more exotic the location of the project, the harder I would work to win it. This approach made me rich in experiences. Although it provided me with a good salary, it did not make me rich moneywise. It also did

OK for my employers, but it did not make them rich either. I regard my personal commitment to becoming the best in industrial sales as an investment. I enjoyed the journey, and I am proud of being the pro I currently am, so I am not regretting my qualification approach.

I came to realize that disqualification can make you rich. To get rich, you have to use all your available resources to their fullest capacity. This does not mean you have to squeeze everything out of every resource, but you have to use the best part of every resource to actualize the financial reward.

My employers might have gained better financial results by tying me to a tighter qualification leash. If they had made me qualify on more financial metrics, I would probably have re-focused to more financially rewarding opportunities. We might not have had so much fun, but our bank accounts would have been happier.

The objective of this book is to become financially rich. It will let you focus on the opportunities that will bring in the most money in the short- and long-term.

We consider disqualification as doing a favor to your income. We can only spend our resources once, so better spend them on the most rewarding tasks. Every disqualification brings us closer to the high-margin projects.

This book is not for the people who are looking for only short-term rewards. We are striving to create businesses that are sustainable and that can withstand the challenges of the future. We look beyond our next pay slip to become richer later.

After completing this book and implementing a solid qualification process, you will be set on a journey to become rich!

Client Pressures

It was Thursday the 22nd of December at 10:00 AM when Frank called me, "Bram, we have a leak in one of our process pipelines that needs repairing." I was puzzled. I had worked on this prospect for six months and had no promising response. Now, just three days before Christmas, Frank calls me.

He continues, "I know you are probably emptying your desk and preparing for your holiday, but I really need you guys down here." I was surprised by how accurate Frank's assumption was about my current activity. I had to return to qualification mode. This is the mode during which you are quartered: the client pulls you in one direction, your company in the other, your entrepreneurial mindset in another direction, and your 'why should I care' mindset goes another.

I looked over my shoulder in the hope of getting an affirming nod or any inspiration that could help, but nobody was in the white room behind me. I decided to make Frank part of my challenge. "Although I am surprised you rang me, I am glad you did. However, your timing could not have been worse. This leak-sealing issue can be resolved by my German colleagues. Those guys really value their Christmas time." I knew I would face a lot of internal objections, but I was up for the challenge.

Frank's company, Exxon Mobil's plant in the Netherlands, was one of my Dream Clients, which I had presented two weeks earlier in my end-of-year update. Besides that, my company had decided that we should focus on leak-sealing. This opportunity would fit in with the sales strategy. It would create a great chance of getting business from this dream client in the future as well.

Together with Frank, I discussed the typical BANT criteria. We set a budget and Frank confirmed that we would get the purchase order immediately. He had the right authority and he felt the urgency himself. We both concluded that fast action was required. I told Frank that I would give him a call back in the afternoon to let him know if we could help him or not.

During this pre-Christmas morning, I was truly convinced that a strategic plan deeply influences the qualification process. It is the direction you are heading which keeps you focused on accepting the right opportunities.

In my case, it was the client who made all the difference. If Frank was with a company that was not on my Dream Client list that day, I would probably have declined. In the end, you are stressing your own resources and you might make promises that you cannot keep. But, for Dream Clients and Future A Clients, you will go the extra mile.

This chapter is about the exceptions to the standard qualification framework. A strict procedure will kill the entrepreneurial spirit of your team. It forces everyone to work the system, instead of using the system. Company guidelines should allow for exceptions in the qualification process. Company culture should encourage exceptions. The exceptions to the qualification process are what will make you rich.

This chapter will deep dive into the exceptions presented by Dream Clients and by Future A Clients. The Future A Clients make you grow long term, while Dream Clients will allow you to generate business with new clients within a shorter time frame.

Another exception presented by your clients is their urgent pain. When the client is in urgent need of your service, you should be able to seize the opportunity to make a difference for them, and you will see the results.

2.1 Qualifying Dream Clients

We all understand the necessity of identifying our Dream Clients for lead generation. However, the relevance of the concept of Dream Clients does not stop at the lead generation process. It will have an impact on other decision-making processes as well, including the qualification process.

When Frank rang me, I knew I had to take this shot. He was on my Dream Client list and the surface qualification criteria (budget, authority, etc.) were met. But, how on earth could I convince the rest of the organization to fulfill the client's wishes?

Since the experience with Frank, I have built a big part of my sales legacy around my "Dream Clients". I encourage the people I coach to do the same. It makes your sales life so much easier and focused.

Advice: create your Dream Clients list to know when to accelerate.

If you know your Dream Clients, you know where to direct your energy. You can target them, approach them through the front door, and identify all the back-door entrances. When the time is right, you will get your shot. In the case of Exxon, it took six months of educating and presenting. During those six months, there was no affirmative response of any kind, but I knew that my patience would be rewarded. The first opportunity presented by a 'hard-to-get' client is never the smoothest. It will put you to some kind of test, but you will accept the challenge because you worked hard to get the chance.

> *Advice: create internal awareness of your Dream Clients.*

If your colleagues know your Dream Clients, they know what makes you run. They can agree or disagree with your choices. They can get used to the idea that they might be working for one of your Dream Clients in the near future. Your colleagues can prepare themselves to take the next step in growing the business.

In the qualification struggle, you will need buy-in from some of your colleagues. Your colleagues will be more motivated to join your battle when they have been part of your journey to win the specific prospect.

You have been discussing your Dream Clients with your colleagues. They might even have helped you gain a seat at the prospect's table. The whole company has a chance to shine with the right project.

> *Advice: tender and execution resources are the main factors when qualifying dream clients.*

The hip-hop artist Marshall B. Mathers (a.k.a. Eminem) sings "You only get one shot, do not miss your chance to blow", as if he was paying tribute to the qualification struggle. A Dream Client is not listed as a one-time success. You identified the Dream Client for its long-term business potential.

The first opportunity presented will not be a perfect match for your company's competencies, or it offers other challenges, like timing. The challenges should not be too difficult to overcome. If we could not have sealed Frank's leak, the door would be slammed in our faces again. It would not reopen and it would smooth the path for our competition. You really get only one chance.

> *Advice: never disqualify opportunities with Dream Clients.*

Declining opportunities that do not fit or cause too much hassle is too easy. The Dream Client should be getting to know you. Inviting you in their purchasing decision opens the door for communication; use this entrance to explain what you CAN do.

In today's business environment, it is unlikely that you have a perfect match. The requested competencies, process, and timeline will most likely not meet your current offer. We have been talking about the client journey for many years now. It is a journey you embark on together. During the journey, you will move closer and closer towards each other as long as you are on the journey together. If you are not embarking on the journey, you will never get anywhere.

> *Advice: educate your Dream Client by participating in tenders.*

You will need a couple of tenders to introduce your Dream Client to your way of working. Together with the previous advice (never disqualify opportunities for Dream Clients), you will be able to present what you CAN offer. When it is not a perfect match in the first tender, it will still start making the Dream Client think.

Benefiting from the Dream Client concept

The concept of Dream Clients is embedded in the acumen of our sales. You should let the concept work for you in the qualification process. The concept forms an exception to the rational factors outlined in traditional qualification frameworks. You will need to create the bypass specifically for Dream Clients. If you start the qualification process for Dream Clients the same way as you would for regular clients, you will miss out on amazing growth potential.

Action: create awareness of Dream Clients.

Within your sales team, you should have a common understanding of who your Dream Clients are. And more importantly, how you serve them differently. Your marketing and sales force puts in a lot of effort to get a business relationship going with the Dream Client. Your qualification process is a result of this effort.

I am not advocating you do everything your dream client asks, but you should be more proactive in letting them know what you CAN do. If an opportunity meets your competencies and you are able to offer a technical solution, you should push to qualify the opportunity.

Action: pick your Dream Clients.

One of the companies I worked with was highly dependent on two large clients in the food industry. These clients sucked up all the manufacturing capacity. Although the shareholders pushed for a more diverse portfolio, all new initiatives to get new clients on board were knocked down during the qualification meetings. Finally, the sales team adopted the Dream Clients concept and pinpointed five Dream Clients. They got approval from the board and from the shareholders that these were Dream Clients. Once the first opportunity came in from one of the five Dream Clients, the capacity was found to convert the opportunity into a contract resulting in an additional big client.

This example shows the importance of getting a commitment from your company before the sales process starts and without commitment, the sales energy will not lead to these Dream Clients. The discussion sends everyone in the right direction from the start.

Action: visualize your Dream Clients.

The names of your Dream Clients should be visible. You should print their names and put them prominently on your wall, mention them in your regular sales team meetings and during the commercial presentations you hold internally.

By sharing the names of your Dream Clients, you keep the concept alive. Once you arrive at the desks of your colleagues to ask for their advice on the new tender of one of your Dream Clients, they will be supportive. If they feel it is just another opportunity, your colleagues will be less likely to support you.

Action: keep disqualifying, also for Dream Clients.

It is not you who will disqualify opportunities with Dream Clients, but you will guide them to a conclusion. This conclusion might be that you are not the right fit. Your Dream Client will try to qualify himself. He will explain why you should offer. He will explain the potential of more business and will outline that he does not have too many alternatives.

All the efforts of the Dream Client to become your client can make you commit to his opportunity. But, in case your organization can really not deliver, you will end up in a tough position. Try to avoid the situation of overpromising since it will backfire on you each time.

Resources are limited and they should be deployed for the right opportunities.

How the Dream Client Fits in the Process

We have learned that rational factors are not the key to qualification success. Some clients require a more entrepreneurial approach. When traditional frameworks tell you to disqualify, you might still want to qualify the opportunities of your Dream Clients. You do not get many chances to start a business relationship and you worked hard towards it.

So, Dream Clients get special treatment. Another group of prospects may be entitled to an exceptional approach as well. You will have ambitions to grow in a different direction. You will want to diversify, which requires a different kind of client. These clients, for sure, will not fit in the current qualification framework. These clients are called the Future AClients. The next section is dedicated to this group of companies and their needs.

2.2 Qualifying Future A Clients

The world is changing rapidly. We are witnessing a shift from fossil fuel to renewable energy, from automation in Industry 3.0 to digitalization in Industry 4.0, and from resource abundance to resource scarcity. This leads to changing clients.

For the majority of my corporate life, I have spent selling within fossil fuel industries. The organizations I worked with wanted to move into renewable industries. They wanted to move from servicing oil and gas assets to windpower assets. This move has a set of challenges that cannot be overcome overnight.

Our company had the same ambition: move into renewables. After doing their homework to pass the minimum competition standards, our sales team jumped into the prospecting game. While the diversification strategy is under development, the first opportunities drip in. The deadline for proposal submission is short and the first few days are already consumed by deciphering the jargon of the new industry.

After the specifications have been deciphered, you will find out that you are missing a lot of competencies and that the other qualification criteria will not be met. You are about to decline because of the complexity, but you have heard about the Future A concept.

The Future A concept is developed to make diversification processes possible. It allows for exceptions to the standard qualification framework. Let me talk you through what it means to adopt the Future A concept.

> *Advice: look out for company diversification needs and align with corresponding Future A Clients.*

The Future A prospect is needed to take your first steps into a new market. You cannot enter a new market without targeting new clients. It is not enough to communicate your desire; you actively have to pursue opportunities. Identifying your Future A Clients streamlines your efforts.

When my previous sales team and I felt the need to broaden our client portfolio into offshore wind, we were actively prospecting a handful of Future A's. We took the initiative to present the new market segment to the management team and mentioned our Future A Clients as examples of target companies. Within a few years, the new market segment was adopted in the company strategy and we had been well introduced in the Future A space already. It took us quite some time to get invited to tender.

Once you are invited to tender, never disqualify. You will learn from the exercise.

> *Advice: when tendering for your Future A, think long term.*

Your Future A audience will speak a different language than you are used to. Tenders are set up differently and the contracting strategy does not seem logical at first. You need to get used to this new type of client.

Going through the tender documents, you will only read about unfamiliar activities. Your organization is not yet equipped to meet the project specifications. Sales need to take the first step. Try to meet the tender specifications and requirements and submit your tender. Disqualification at this stage will kill your future chance of business.

> *Advice: only disqualify once with your Future A.*

The first time you are invited to tender by one of your Future A Clients you can decide to decline. You need to take the opportunity to educate your prospect. By declining, you can open up the line of communication and try to explain your added value. Try to establish an understanding of what they can ask from you. Preferably, also educate the Future A Client on how they can buy from you.

If you disqualify more than once, you are thrown backward a couple of years in your prospecting cycle. You will need to work hard to get a third tender request, which might never come.

> *Advice: 1 in 5 Dream Clients should be on your Future A list.*

The difference between Dream Clients and Future A Clients is the product /market combination. Dream Clients operate in familiar markets, while Future A clients are active in new territory. You will need more Dream Clients to make you rich in the short term, but you have the obligation to look long term as well.

Qualification of opportunities from Dream Clients and opportunities from Future A Clients differ as well. Opportunities of Dream Clients require competencies you already possess, while for Future A Clients, you will need to acquire new competencies. Tendering for Future A Clients requires a lot of effort, so it is better to not get taken away by market trends. In the example of offshore wind, you can easily be dragged away by all the nice market forecasts. But you can only use your resources once. You need to find a balance in your tendering activities.

> *Advice: disqualify tenders that require a short tender reaction time.*

To prepare a solid tender submission for your Future A, you will need more time than for other tenders. You can also question the intentions of your Future A prospect. Do they only want your submission to benchmark or to please the chasing salesperson? If deadlines are too short, you will need to decline. You cannot afford to spend an enormous amount of time if you are unable to prepare a solid initial bid.

Benefiting from Future A qualification.
Disqualification makes you rich. Projects with Future A companies will not make you rich in the short term but will offer business continuity in the long term. You will need to invest time and effort to get new market segments going.

Action: find the obvious area of client diversification.

Within your company, there are people with strong opinions and people with a lot of experience. These people will make change happen. Listen to their stories and try to identify for what industry they would support your opportunities.

Investigate the new industries and create a high-level assumption on the kinds of tenders that you will be focusing on. Communicate this within your company and prepare people that these tenders will be the result of the diversification process. At an early stage, start preparing everyone for a different kind of qualification process.

Action: picture the long-term consequence of current tenders.

Tenders have to fit a plan. Tenders from Future A should be well prepared. You should prevent being invited for tenders that do not serve the company's ambition. At the qualification meeting, you need to explain the project and its immediate consequences. You also need to picture what journey you are embarking on as a company.

The first tender will not be profitable, but you will learn a lot. The profit margins will increase with the next projects. You will learn skills that can be marketed differently, but these changes might also affect how the business is structured. During the qualification meeting, you will have to address all these future consequences.

How Future A fits in the process.

Every qualification process needs room to deviate from the standard framework. If you stick to the traditional qualification factors, you might miss out on opportunities. You need to think of the future. You might not become rich by qualifying opportunities for the future, but you should allow for diversification to create business continuity and to create more room for future growth.

In this chapter, we covered exceptions that will boost mid-term business growth (Dream Client) and long-term potential (Future A). These delayed chances to become rich should be regarded as a long-term investment. Every business should allow for these exceptions.

The exceptions should be integrated into the qualification process. The qualification decision should always be a consensus.

So, we have covered the long-term and mid-term exceptions, but we need to make one more exception. One that might make you rich on shorter notice. The deviation for urgent opportunities will be the subject of the next section. Clients might have immediate needs that can create leverage for more business or generate instant gains.

2.3 Qualification for Urgency

One of the four big Korean shipyards was about to release a new build FPSO vessel, when it found that the flare tip needed replacement. The end client refused to sign off before the flare tip was replaced. The tugboats were already in the port to guide the FPSO vessel into open waters.

The management of the shipyard instructed its external construction manager to solve the issue as soon as possible, whatever the costs. The British construction manager felt the pressure of the complete company, while he was already exhausted. The last few weeks had been very frenzied to get to this point. He had already packed his bags to return to the UK right after releasing the FPSO vessel.

The construction manager desperately looked through his inbox, searching for an email he had received a few weeks ago. He knew he had received an email from a service provider specialized in flare tip replacements without requiring large cranes. He did not respond to the email and thought he would not need this kind of service. He finally found the email and called the sender.

I did not expect to receive a call from a Korean phone number, but I answered the call. I felt the pain of the construction manager immediately. I felt sorry for him and wanted to help. After a few questions it became clear that my support would be well rewarded.

My standard qualification framework turned red on available resources. The commercial process was already hard to complete at short notice, but mobilizing crew and equipment on very short notice was even more challenging. On the other hand, I realized that the gains would be immense.

During this process, I found out that the urgency exception should be in every qualification decision. You will be able to strengthen your relationship with current clients or seize immediate financial rewards.

The urgency exception is the topic here to help clients in your current market.

> *Advice: integrate urgency into your qualification process.*

In all B2B environments, unexpected events will present themselves. It is the supply chain that needs to support clients to solve immediate challenges. Your qualification process prescribes to decline these opportunities, but this is a little shortsighted.

Declining clients in need's opportunities will open the door for competition, it will leave money on the table, and you will miss out on strengthening your relationship with existing clients.

The escalation process is required to make proper decisions and to get management commitment early in the process.

Addressing the urgency exception will fuel the sales team's entrepreneurial spirit. The sales team will feel that there is an opportunity to serve clients in need. If they do not have this feeling, they will decline too quickly.

> *Advice: let your client set the budget.*

Your client in pain understands that you have to put in a lot of extra effort to meet his request on short notice. He actually needs to qualify himself and he knows that. A salesperson might get dollar signs in his eyes; however, you are on a thin line. By letting your client in pain set the budget, you eliminate the risk of crossing the line.

> *Advice: be honest about the possibilities.*

You can explain your challenges and make your client part of your struggle. Be honest and do not exaggerate your challenges. You are in the business of helping clients, not to get your emotional needs met. Honestly explain what the major challenges are and what the project risks are. If you conclude that you cannot help the client soon enough, let them know.

You should be able to help the client, even if you are not able to provide the service yourself. By now, you are understanding their challenge and you are able to point them in the right direction. There is always a solution, and you know the challenge best. Even if you have to guide the client to your competitor, you should do so and support the client in addressing the pitfalls.

Keep supporting your client, even when he is not buying from you.

> *Advice: be very careful to qualify for urgency with Future A companies.*

Future A companies are operating in an industry you do not know. They might have a different understanding of urgency. You do not understand all the mechanisms in the market yet. By accepting an urgent opportunity, you will be dragged in the swamp of the new market. The risk of long-term damage is present at every point of your project.

Benefiting from implementing urgency into qualification.

The objective of implementing the urgency card into the qualification process should not be the financial reward. The objective should be to allow the process to be different in case one of your clients is in need. Your business is built on helping clients. If you help clients in need, they will likely remain clients in good times.

Action: empower the sales team to support Future A Clients with urgent pain.

Your sales force should be mandated to support clients in need. The process should enable them to take a qualification shortcut. The urgency shortcut does not need to be promoted, but the salesperson should feel that there is an option to help the client in need.

Some company cultures do not allow for this "fast-track service". Salespersons feel that they have to decline the requests from clients in need. This will potentially hurt the relationship with clients. Your organization should help clients in good and in bad times. The process should allow for this exception.

Action: draw up an escalation process and train those involved.

After your client indicates their need for support on short notice, the escalation process should be defined. Time is of the essence and fast decision making is part of the process. By following the standard process, you will lose real opportunities to win time.

Experienced people, or people who have already been with the organization for a long time know the shortest way to find a solution. However, they can take this route only a few times before it loses its power. By implementing a predefined process, everybody involved knows what to do. Who is making the decision to help and who will execute after the main decision is taken?

Action: roll out the urgency process to your A clients

The urgency process does not need to be a secret process. You can communicate the process to your A clients. Explain the reasons for designing the process and explain in what circumstances this process will be followed. Your client will feel special and recognizes that you are there to support them in good and in bad times. They will try to keep you on board since they know that their projects can take unexpected turns.

How does the urgency exception fit in the qualification process?

We have learned that the urgent requests of clients do not fit the standard qualification process. Just like special requests of Dream Clients and your Future A Clients, you will need to differ from your standard qualification framework.

Time is of the essence when the client is in short-term pain. If you can help this client in a timely manner, they will reward you financially and with future business.

Implement the urgency shortcut into your qualification process to empower your sales team to be prepared and to show your A Clients that you really care.

We covered all the exceptions that could be presented by our current and future clients. But what should be included as a minimum in the standard framework? That is what we will cover in the next section.

2.4 Standard Qualification Frameworks

This book is designed to bridge the gap between the theory and practical sales environment. From experience, I know that most sales teams are aware of the importance of lead and opportunity qualification. However, they have never completely implemented a standard framework. I believe that it is because the sales teams are afraid they will lose the power to deviate.

I promote the use of standard frameworks and try to show where the struggles are. The wins are in the struggles. Sales teams can make a difference if they understand the struggles and how to use them to their and the client's advantage.

This chapter of the book provides insights into the different clients and their need to interrupt your standard process. It also shows some basic elements of your standard framework, and these basic elements are subject to your client's intent. That is why this section is included in the "Client Struggle" chapter.

> *Advice: keep the qualification process within the sales team.*

Qualifying opportunities is a decision that involves more people than just the commercial team. In most companies, production, engineering, and other operational departments will also have a say in the qualification decision. They will need to execute after the award. These internal struggles will be the topic of Chapter 3.

In this chapter, I will outline the criteria that will make the opportunity qualified from a commercial perspective. The sales team will qualify based on the intention of the client. Has the client the right budget, authority, necessity, and many other factors? These factors should be determined within sales. Other internal powers will use the factors to push their agenda, which is not preferred in the commercial process.

Make the rest of the company part of your journey. Explain the criteria you are using and those you are not using. Show them that you use the same framework consistently and what deviations you can accept and under what circumstances. You will create awareness within your organization but keep control.

> *Advice: use the opportunity qualification process to streamline sales and execution capacity.*

The lead and opportunity qualification process indicates the level of success of your marketing and sales engine. The number of disqualified opportunities is an important metric to measure. It indicates how well your organization fits into the market and how well the sales engine is performing.

I am not telling you that you should keep the number as low as possible. Some companies need to qualify hard to find the sweet spots. Those companies sell on scarcity, which can be a highly rewarding strategy.

Other companies might need to disqualify because of executing capacity. If that is the same case over a longer period of time, companies should consider decreasing their sales engine or increasing the executing capacity.

How to benefit from a standard framework?

Standard frameworks have been designed as a guideline. They are created to standardize the qualification process. They provide clear instructions to the salespeople in the trenches as to what opportunities to chase and which to decline. Many companies have implemented a standard qualification framework or a lead-scoring program.

Scoring programs are designed to allow for periodic or seasonal changes. Less high-scoring opportunities can still be qualified in times that are less busy.

Although I am not a big fan, there are a lot of benefits to implementing a standard framework. Make sure you allow for deviations as presented in this chapter and elsewhere in this book.

Action: define your standard qualification framework.

The obvious first step is to design your standard framework. If you start from scratch, it will be an exhausting exercise. There are just too many variables to consider. It is better to start with a standard framework, such as BANT, MEDDIC, MEDDPICC, PMAR, CHAMP,

GPCTBA/C&I, FAINT, or ANUM. That so many standard frameworks are floating around indicates the complexity of the process.

I would select one that you like and start to implement it. While implementing and adjusting the framework to your needs, make sure you capture all relevant exceptions in the process. You do not want the framework to be leading the decision process. There should always be room for creativity and entrepreneurship.

I will not go into details on all the different frameworks. You should google them and find out for yourself. For the sake of simplicity, I will give you two options. If you want a straightforward framework, choose BANT (Budget, Authority, Needs, Timeline), which is the oldest framework I know of. If you want to take the most advanced one and you are willing to take more variables into consideration, you can choose the GPTCBA/C&I (Goals, Plans, Timeline, Challenges, Budget, Authority/Negative Consequences, and Positive Implications) framework. I believe that it is the most complete. The latter one allows for more interpretation and requires more business feeling.

Action: create a "how to work with us" guideline for your clients.

When you select your basic framework, you can play around with it. You can make your client part of the qualification process. The concept of mutual qualification can be used, which acknowledges that both the selling company as well as the buying company are in qualification mode. Sales is trying to pass the qualification of the client. Why not let the client qualify for his project with the salesperson?

The buyer often explains what they require to accept the offer. The other way around would work as well. The seller could indicate in what circumstance it is willing to use its resources to help the client.

Your discussions will be much more constructive if you adopt the mutual qualification process.

Action: make AI and automation take over part of the qualification process.

It may sound scary, but Artificial Intelligence, automation, and machine learning are finding their way into the sales process. We might dislike it, but we cannot stop this development. If you have adopted a standard qualification framework, there will be a machine that can take the CRM data and make the qualification decision on your behalf.

The qualification process will be more rational if we let computers take over. This might not be a bad thing after all. It creates more transparency for clients, which adds value on its own.

How does the traditional qualification framework fit into the modern qualification process?

I am not here to create a revolution. I am here to allow you to benefit from the qualification process. The standard frameworks kill entrepreneurship and hurt your company culture. They will hinder growing relationships with existing clients and will obstruct future growth.

To win future business, you will need to act flexibly and quickly. Your processes should be aligned with the world around you, which offers you opportunities that do not fit within standard frameworks. Nevertheless, the standard frameworks are a good starting point. It requires the salesperson to think of the standard qualification questions before considering escalating an exception.

The choice for a qualification framework greatly depends on the choice of allowing for exceptions. If you allow for exceptions and encourage entrepreneurship, I advise adopting the most straightforward system. In my opinion, BANT is the most user-friendly system. It covers the basics, which is enough to qualify or disqualify most opportunities.

If you do not want to provide the escape routes (Dream Clients, Future A, urgency) to your sales team, you are better off selecting a more complex qualification system. Be prepared for some more resistance from your sales team since it will provide them with a more labor-intensive procedure.

2.5 Summary

I started this chapter with a story about a client in need. He presented me with a challenge and an internal conflict. If I accepted his challenge and took the business opportunity, I would make a very nice sale, I would create the chance to start a long-term relationship and would make my prospect happy. On the other hand, it would require me to battle internally. I would need to convince my German colleagues to change their Christmas plans. I would need to persuade many people within my management. It would cost me a lot of stress.

By not accepting the challenge, I would have lost nothing. The prospect was not a client of ours, so we would not have lost any business that we had before. I would just have said 'no' and granted myself and my German colleagues a quiet Christmas period. My manager would not have noticed and if he did, I could have used parts of a standard qualification framework to defend my decision.

Every salesperson will make a different decision when presented by this conflict. Typical salespeople are presented with these kind of opportunities several times a year. These circumstances will accelerate your growth into a new business or a lucrative short-term business. It is the company leadership who will reward or punish the salesperson's actions.

It is not in my character to leave good opportunities on the table. I choose the hard way. I choose to help the client and to fight the internal battle. The project was a success. The client was happy that his problem was being solved. My manager was happy with the nice extra end-of-year business. And, even my German colleagues were proud that they pulled it off. The client invited us to establish a frame agreement for further leak-sealing business, which presented me with another qualification challenge. The project took a toll on many within the organization. Not everybody was enthusiastic when presented with more of those challenges.

This lesson teaches us that our clients can present us with nice opportunities. However, we have to deal with internal pressures. The extent of internal pressures or the options to put these pressures to rest will indicate your level of success. The next chapter will cover your internal struggle and how everyone can benefit from these internal pressures to win more and better business.

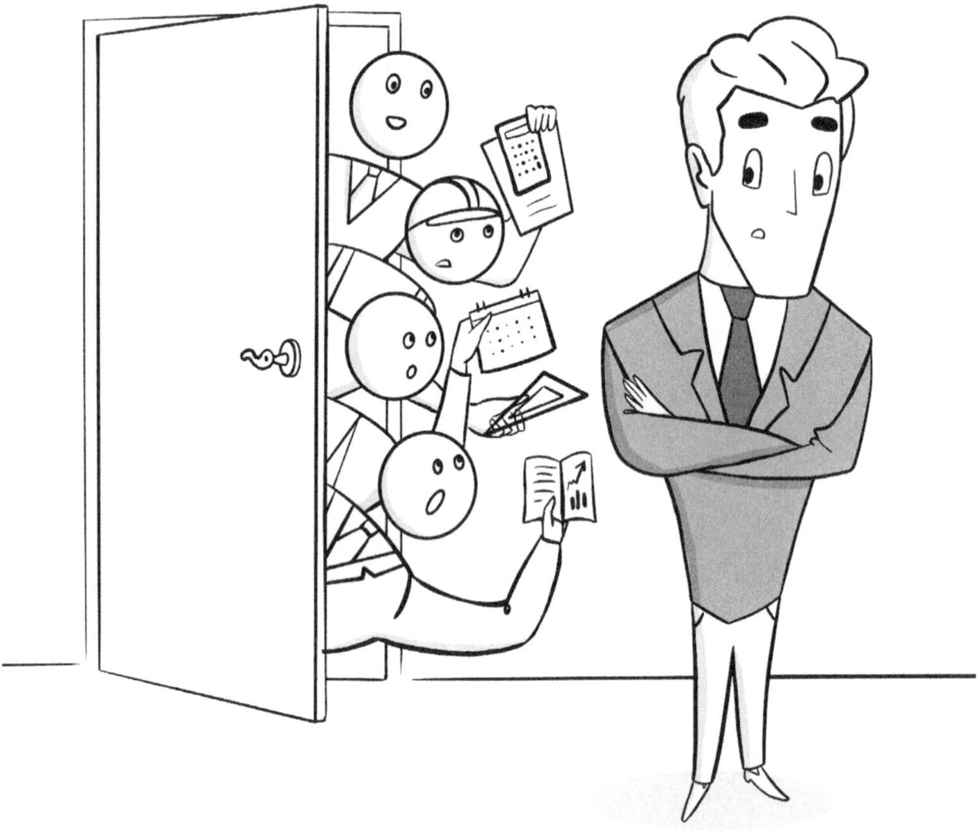

Internal Pressures

The number one reason for salespeople to leave their job is not compensation. It is not possible career opportunities. The number one reason for salespeople to leave their job is management effectiveness and company culture. Studies show that there is a correlation between the number of sales-related activities and the level of job satisfaction. The more salespeople can spend on actually selling, the happier they are.

The average salesperson spends less than 30% of their time actually selling. The rest of their time is filled with planning activities and internal matters. An often-heard complaint within the sales teams I coach is, "it is easier to sell to clients than to my colleagues".

Every new project that is brought in is hammered down along with the motivation of the salesperson. The salesperson has spent a lot of time winning the deal and is excited about the contract they have just signed. This excitement decreases when preparing the handover and is completely eliminated by the end of the handover meeting.

The future project manager asks questions like: "Why are there no clear milestones defined in the contract?" and "Can you arrange for more time, because of what you have promised …?". You know the drill. It will take a couple of months before the project manager has the same level of excitement as you had yesterday.

As a result, the salesperson's leash is shortened by squeezing his qualification freedom even further. If we do not start empowering salespeople to convert their natural drive for finding new opportunities, our businesses will lose their acting power. This chapter provides guidance for turning the internal pressures into drivers for growth.

This is what happened with one of my clients. Peter, the most senior salesperson at a machine manufacturer, received a Request for Quotation in his mailbox for shot peening of turbine blades. This is a process to harden components to increase their lifetime. It had been ten years since the machining company was successful with this service, but Peter felt there was still a good market for it.

The appetite for this service was not huge, however, current business was slow. After Peter discussed it with his client, he decided to give it a go internally. He started his qualification round to get feedback from his colleagues.

He discovered there was an appetite to restart this kind of service. Peter presented what was offered in the past and how that service had been very successful. Since the factory floor needed additional work, his operational colleagues were easily convinced.

The current director, the son of the founder, found out about the opportunity. He injected himself into the discussion. Shot peening was not part of his big plan. He had a strong desire to decline the opportunity since it did not fit with his ambitions with the company.

Where operations could fill the production schedule, it was the director who blocked the opportunity because he was unable to see the project potential.

Where there is friction, things move. In this chapter, I will outline how to benefit from the internal pressures. I will guide you through the jungle of corporate life. You will not lose the feeling of being required to sell twice (to your client and to your colleagues), but you will get the tools to get the best out of the internal experience.

3.1 The Influence of Appetite

In 2012, the oil and gas market was very promising. My company was growing fast, and we could select our opportunities freely. We only had to raise our hands and work was thrown at us. We wanted to work on more exciting projects all the time. When we were requested to perform an unusual job offshore Libya, we were interested right away.

One job involved the installation of living quarters at a platform where there was no accommodation available. The project took place offshore Libya, which was not the friendliest place to visit at that time. The client was not the most experienced offshore operator, and as a result, we had to take on many more responsibilities than we were used to. One of the things we were taking into our scope was the transport of the module from the manufacturer in the Netherlands to Libya, including loading the vessel, chartering the vessel, and customs. We had never offered these services before.

If we had been asked to perform the qualification process one year before or one year later, we would have declined. But when the project passed our desk, we felt that we could do everything. We were very ambitious and wanted to have more excitement in our projects. Our appetite was big, and we accepted the challenge, which turned out to be successful.

Within a company's lifetime, the appetite for business changes. It is often referred to as the risk appetite. Risks are inherent to doing business. In opportunity qualification, the appetite for risks affects the decision. This appetite can change every day.

In international standard guidelines (e.g. ISO 31000), risk appetite is described as the "amount and type of risk that an organization is prepared to pursue, retain or take". We need to understand that this can change periodically. It can even change overnight, which makes it an important factor in the qualification process.

There are five levels of risk appetite: averse, minimal, cautious, open, and hungry.

> *Advice: identify the level of risk appetite on a quarterly basis.*

Business changes, and so does the appetite for the type of business you are pursuing. When the opportunity is not sexy, with a limited lead score, and not on your Dream Clients or Future A lists, and it falls within the lower categories of risk appetite (e.g. average, minimal or cautious) there are good reasons for disqualifying the opportunity.

Company management should understand the risk they are willing to take at a particular time. If the risk appetite is not changing a lot, there is no need to perform the periodic review, but if it is, you should. Salespeople should understand what is driving the risk appetite. If they do not understand, they will regard the company as unstable, and this will reflect on their clients.

> *Advice: link the risk appetite to ambition.*

In the next section, the influence of ambition is described. Ambition focuses on the longer term, while the risk appetite is the reflection of today's mood. By using ambition to explain the appetite for risk, people will understand your reasoning.

The world is changing rapidly, new industries are formed, and new companies are created. These companies often need to grow quickly. The faster they can scale up, the bigger their initial investments will be. These companies have a real appetite and are willing to take on exceptional levels of risk, as long as it fits the ambitions of their investors.

However, there are more traditional companies than new ones. Daimler is currently the largest truck and bus manufacturer in the world based on revenue. It has a history that goes back to the 19th century. Their current owners are happy with the fruits of their investments. Business continuity and stability are more important than growth. When qualification decisions are made, the appetite for risk is low. Daimler issues a "risk and opportunity" report to keep its stakeholders up to date on its appetite.

> *Advice: journal the issues that have an impact on appetite.*

They say your customers' last buying experience is your biggest competition. The same is true for risk appetite within your own company. All actors in the qualification struggle have picked up positive and negative experiences in their lives that they bring to the table. The most recent experiences outweigh past experiences. Bad experiences outweigh positive experiences.

By journaling the 'trash' in people's minds, you will be able to mitigate the perceived risks.

When Joe was suffering a lot of additional costs when working on a South African project, he brought this experience into the qualification process. This is not a bad thing; you only need to be aware of the cause of Joe's thinking to improve the qualification decision.

> *Advice: analyze the qualification trends within your company.*

There are many variables when making a qualification decision. This is the main reason for this book. Many of the variables are directly generated from the perceptions people have. Strong opinions will influence the qualification process and other people's opinions might be integrated in the process by manipulation.

When Joe left, it was easier to qualify for South African projects again. The trend moved towards more appetite for South African projects. By identifying the trends, you will be able to steer them in line with your expected next opportunities. When you feel that there will be a lot of opportunities requiring third-party engineering, you can take the initiative to start educating people. Once the new opportunity arises, the appetite to adopt this additional risk will be higher.

Benefiting from appetite.

I hate to lose opportunities because I misjudged the willingness to take risks. In all projects, there are some levels of risk. More risky projects fuel my day. I am hungry to take risks, which is true for many people in the sales profession. We are often referred to as opportunists for good reason.

We should keep this opportunism within our sales teams. The number one killer for opportunism is the disqualification based on appetite. Instead, use the appetite to the benefit of all.

Action: create awareness of the impact of business appetite.

The organization should be focused on the projects where the most value can be added. It is essential that everyone understands the importance of this focus. We all have the responsibility to use the resources within our sphere of influence effectively, and focus is an irreplaceable part of the game.

If the business appetite remains within the board room or within operational departments, it cannot be used to steer the commercial efforts in the right direction. It will eventually have side effects, such as a demotivated workforce, strategic diversion, and a waste of resources.

Action: start communicating on business appetite.

As the appetite for increased business or risks changes periodically, we need to keep communicating about it. The factors that influence the appetite can be predicted by experienced people and should be shared, formally or informally.

When Jack approached his boss to go after a new opportunity together with their Vietnamese partner in December 2019, his boss let him think about the business appetite of all the people involved. Jack's upper management was based in the US, where they were already cleaning their desks for Christmas. The Vietnamese partner was closing in on the Chinese New Year celebrations. Although these celebrations took place in February, a lot of people would already be returning to their families at the beginning of January. The momentum from Jack's initiative resulted in disqualification.

There are many factors involved in changing appetite. The seasonality of the opportunity is one, but you need to also think of more business strategies or business planning factors, such as company ownership changes, operational capacity planning, liquidity matters, etc.

Not all things can be communicated in memos or during "official" meetings. Nevertheless, it makes sense to communicate to manage the expectations of the sales team. What they considered adding to the strategy yesterday might no longer contribute today. To keep the sales team focused, a sense of the current business appetite should be shared.

Action: step on the right wave.

The salesperson, together with his client, can catch the right wave of business appetite. There are occasions when a salesperson has the chance to take the next step with a client, but momentum is the main obstruction.

When my company was developing a system to replace components inside a wind turbine, it was hard to make the investment decision. In talks with clients, we found a way to catch the next internal wave within our mother company to get this investment decision over the line.

This opportunity will not arise for every tender, but situations will arise in which the business appetite will be in line with what you and your client want to achieve. Take advantage of the internal appetite to get buy-in from your colleagues.

How does the business appetite fit into the qualification process?

In this section, examples are given of how appetite affects the qualification decision. They all come down to benefiting from internal trends. It is the appetite that will grow the company and give it direction. The appetite has the power to accelerate the business or slow it down.

The appetite is affected by many factors, some of which are more tangible than others. In the examples of seasonal changes to appetite, the business is slowed down. In strategic scenarios, you often have the chance to let your client benefit from the new appetite, for example, to enter a new type of business.

The understanding of the changing appetite should be companywide to manage expectations and to commercialize the appetite. It is frustrating to find out that your new opportunity does not fit within the company's current appetite. You could have invested your time better in something that would have fit.

Appetite is closely connected to the level of ambition. The ambition of the business changes frequently during its lifetime. It often has to do with changing ownership, changing management, or strong external factors. The next chapter will dive deeply into the impact of company ambition on the qualification process.

3.2 Organizational Ambition

In 2020, a sales manager of a small industrial service provider launched the 10 * 10 * 10 goals for his sales team. The company was making 10 million USD in revenue, and within 10 years they would multiply by 10. This goal sets an ambitious direction. Some people fell off their chairs (from laughter or from being startled). It was meant to inspire people and to provide a sense of excitement.

The sales manager personally committed his time to this goal. He understood that he could not realize this goal without chasing a different kind of opportunity. He kept repeating his goal, so he became accountable to the rest of the organization, which soon adopted the same ambition.

During the sales manager's spring break in 2021, a member of his team presented an opportunity that would instantly add more than 20 million of revenue spread over the next three years. The opportunity would introduce the company to a different league of projects.

The sales manager reacted very positively and decided to support it fully after his holiday. On the first day after he came into the office, a call with the partner was scheduled and cooperation was agreed upon. They would tender together and take responsibility for their own scope.

If the sales representative had reported to his manager before the 10 * 10 * 10 goal was set, he would not have received support from him. Since the manager was personally committed to this goal, he had no other option than to support the opportunity. The company's ambition together with the sales manager's ambition resulted in a qualified opportunity.

The example shows that if an opportunity taps into the ambitions of a company or individuals, it will be qualified. Most projects are within the comfort zone of the company. In that case, the opportunity is qualified. However, to get rich, you will need extraordinary projects that require a different kind of energy. This energy is generated from ambition.

> *Advice: identify and communicate the long-term ambition and vision.*

Although it may seem obvious to share your long-term strategy, a study from IBM Watson Media indicates that "72 percent of employees do not fully understand their company's strategy". If your sales team does not know the long-term goals, it is hard for them to tap into them. They will be struggling to find the right opportunities to meet that goal.

By not communicating the long-term ambition, you leave money on the table. Your sales team is bound to attract opportunities that are the same as the current project portfolio. More exciting opportunities are not pursued and opportunities with Dream Clients might be overlooked.

> *Advice: streamline corporate goals with the company purpose.*

It is a trendy topic to have the company's purpose high on the agenda. The "why" of the business to which the employees and (future) clients can relate. By matching the corporate goals to the company's purpose, you will motivate salespersons to look beyond the obvious.

The purpose translates the revenue goals into something more tangible. Creativity to find new opportunities will be sparked and exciting opportunities will be the result.

The qualification process becomes more flexible by including the purpose. The projects that contribute to the feeling of purpose are very attractive. The prospect will feel the enthusiasm and drive of your organization towards their project. They feel that they will benefit from having your company on board, instead of others for which it is just another "day at the office".

> *Advice: disqualify hard if the opportunity does not fit the corporate ambition.*

In industrial segments, we have seen clear shifts away from fossil fuel, or away from labor-intensive opportunities. By actively changing the project portfolio, you can allow the transition towards a new corporate ambition. You disqualify opportunities that do not match your long-term ambition.

In flourishing times, this is easy to do. In less flourishing times, making the choice to not offer the service is more difficult. It should be a management decision to disqualify opportunities today that would have been offered a year ago. However, this disqualification is required to meet your desired market space in the future.

When an engineering firm tried to move away from the engineering business, they needed to consistently communicate the message to their clients. The inquiries for engineering services kept pouring into their funnels. Their clients were expecting a commercial offer, but the firm declined the opportunities and tried to convince them to request broader packages, which would include engineering in combination with the execution of the final project.

The salespeople should be made aware of a change like this and of the chance that their opportunities might be disqualified in the future. The sales manager has to look at his past projects periodically to find the projects for which the qualification would currently be questionable. Once identified, he should share this with the team and provide clear reasoning.

Benefiting from Ambition

Ambition is the best fertilizer for growing new business. It is what makes your business flourish, and it is what sets you apart from the competition. Using the ambition to qualify for the right opportunities to motivate people makes sense and it will allow for exponential growth.

Action: translate ambition to project examples.

We set an ambition to increase business in the renewable industry. We were all excited to get started. We even implemented it into our talent acquisition program, which boosted the interest of engineers to start working with us. We all understood the importance of the new market and agreed that this would be the future.

The sales team soon came to me with questions. First of all, what was our track record in the new industry? I explained that the track record was limited. Their next question was what projects to focus on. Since there were no previous project experience, it was hard for them to know what services to offer. Besides that, the industry was organized differently from the ones we served before. This affected the type of prospect to chase.

It required many brainstorming sessions internally and a lot of sales organization before we came up with a list of services we could offer. Once the list was created, the new opportunities were floating in just in time before we lost motivation to target this new industry.

Action: create clear (dis)qualification reasons for changed ambitions.

Clients might become confused if you tell them that the service you offered three years before will no longer be offered. You need to help the client understand the changed ambition. He should not get the feeling that it is his fault you are changing course.

By creating clear disqualification factors and providing reasoning, your sales team is better equipped for the next client conversation.

The opposite is also true. The opportunities you might have declined in the past, you now want to chase. Your prospect might not even request your offer because he feels that you are not interested in their business. By providing solid reasoning for changing the desired project portfolio, you will be able to convince the client.

Action: create an internal communication plan to share the corporate ambition.

Management should climb onto the soapbox periodically to present or repeat the corporate ambition. Even when the ambitions and the corporate goals remain unchanged, management should address the employees. My advice is to choose a monthly interval for this type of internal communication. The medium can be different: presenting in person, a recorded video message, or even an email might do the job. The communication should be personal and predictable.

By not communicating according to a plan, you will create anxiety when the next update presentation is announced. People will feel that there are changes coming. This will trigger a reaction that often has a negative impact on the company's effectiveness.

How Ambition Fits into the Process?

In the qualification process, the sales team will be supported when the entire company is on the same page with the company direction. The qualification of new opportunities will be smoother and people will understand the disqualification of opportunities that were executed in the past. So, in general, communicating on ambition will smooth the qualification process tremendously.

Transparency is vital in the current corporate environment. Clients want to understand the direction of our companies. They want to have predictable partners to solve their business needs. The ambition of a company plays a vital part. Ambition has proved to be very flexible. It can develop over time due to changes within the company and to the changing environment.

One thing is clear, ambition influences qualification. If the new opportunity meets all qualification framework criteria it can still not be in line with corporate long-term ambition. If the project portfolio allows, or when the drive for change is really big, the opportunity might still be disqualified.

The contrary is true as well. When not all standard qualification criteria are met, the company can still decide to qualify the opportunity to meet its ambition.

The corporate ambition offers space for the salesperson and his client to streamline the opportunity with what the company wants to provide. This will boost the long-term relationship with the client and revenues from these opportunities.

In short, the appetite and ambition might be contradictory, but by combining both perspectives you get a clear impression of the opportunities that should be chased today and the opportunities that are right for the future.

The rest of this chapter will be devoted to the internal resources and to the project potential.

3.3 Project Execution Constraints

Every Monday morning, I attended the resource planning meeting. All my operational colleagues were exaggerating their utilization. If they had room for additional projects, they were "totally out of work" and if they were full, they were "stressing" their resources. It seemed that there was no middle. It seemed that they never operated at a steady pace for long.

During those meetings, I sat across from the general manager listening to the department managers' stories. It was hard to keep up with all the different messages. There was always a lot of context blurring the conversation. Often, I just disconnected from the conversation. I was physically present, but mentally I was in a different place.

I was enjoying the coffee and the break from the sales team pushing their opportunities. My agenda was different. I had a full pipeline of opportunities. If I mentioned them during these meetings, they were pulled out of context. The qualification process would be hijacked by all the operational people involved. Only the super nice opportunities would be qualified.

If one thing became clear to me during those meetings, it was the reason to clearly separate sales from operations. Where sales wants to get as many projects in, it is up to the operational managers to find a balance between too many projects and boredom. The general manager was at the meeting to be the referee, but the actual referee should be the qualification process.

The qualification process forms the balance between sales and operations.

The quality of the execution is what drives future business. Clients will return and provide referrals if they are happy with the execution of their project. Your organization should always focus on delivering the best quality possible. It can only do so if there are enough resources available at the right time.

You have a double role. You have to match the opportunities with the internal resource planning, and you have to fit in opportunities in gaps in the internal resource planning. Your communication skills are required to see where there is room for optimization. You work closely together with your client and your operational colleagues to streamline resources and expectations.

> *Advice: use your pipeline to flatten the resource utilization factors.*

"We cannot accept this opportunity, because our engineers deserve a holiday", or "Why are we not getting more orders? Our warehouse is running full?" are examples of short-term peaks or lows in the perception of your operational colleagues. You can use those extremes to fit in the right opportunities at the right time.

You indicate that you care about the quality of the work performed and the well-being of your operational colleagues. You indicate that you take their concerns seriously and that you are working towards a steady flow of work.

The overview of your pipeline will provide enough input to put the fears of your colleagues to rest. Share the opportunities that fit into their current struggles. Add new long-term opportunities if the operational departments are working on deadlines. Add short-term opportunities if they experience a shortfall in workload.

> *Advice: provide clarity on your pipeline visually.*

The pipeline you are using in sales is probably not clear for operational people. You have to indicate the factor of time into your visual display of the pipeline. Your typical pipeline focuses on the opportunity stage, where you move clients towards a contract. Your operational colleagues want clarity on when resources are required for these new opportunities.

Most CRM graphs do not provide the complete picture. More integrated solutions connected to and Enterprise Resource System (e.g. SAP) might meet the information requirements of your colleagues, but it is better if sales presents their figures.

Depending on what you are selling, different resources are required at different stages of the project. In the startup phase, you will require engineering resources, at later stages you will need procurement and fabrication, and onsite construction services at the end. By using a typical (average) project turnover division, you should be able to plot the revenue of the project over a certain period and indicate what resources are required at what point in time. You should always present a weighted forecast (revenue x probability) to provide an accurate overview.

The clarity of information defines the level of support of your qualification process. More pressures will be introduced by your operational colleagues when they are unclear about the approaching workload. This feeling makes sense since they do not like to be surprised by a sudden peak, which they cannot answer without sacrificing quality or employee satisfaction.

> *Advice: find out what the personal preference is of your operational colleagues.*

People are more motivated to support projects when they feel personally connected to them. People can be motivated by a great project outcome, by the (type of) client, or by the size of the contract. If sales is aware of the personal motivators of their colleagues, they can more easily get the support to get the qualification outcome they want.

In 2016, things were booming. Our order book was full, and everyone was pushing their limits to get the projects done. When my Middle East sales rep presented a project in Israel, nobody was interested in supporting it until he started talking to Douglas, who recently joined our company as project manager. Apparently, he had roots in Israel but had never visited the country. When he became aware of the new opportunity, he was very excited and personally convinced the rest of the organization that we should quote for the project. We did quote, won, and Douglas traveled to Israel as the project manager.

This is one example of how to involve people who are personally connected to the opportunity. During my career, I was surprised how the opportunity could motivate people to get it qualified. A project was scheduled to be executed close to a full moon party in Thailand, which was on someone's bucket list. A client who was in the same city as where the favorite football player moved to was another attraction. The list goes on and on.

The space between business objectives and personal objectives can be used to get your opportunities qualified, even when the odds are against the opportunity initially.

Benefiting from the project execution factor during the qualification process.

Action: benefit from timing.

Never ask colleagues to qualify for an extraordinary opportunity on a Monday or Friday morning. On a Monday, the chances are that the organization is tied up with planning calls and might be overwhelmed by the presented workload. On a Friday, deadlines are often set. Deadline stress changes the perception of available capacity.

Typically, you start your qualification process on a Tuesday and try to get a conclusion before Thursday 2:00 PM. Tuesdays and Wednesdays are used to understand all obstructions and during a qualification meeting on Thursday, it all starts making sense. People start looking to the new challenge as an opportunity.

Action: try to understand all objections and address them proactively.

It takes some time to mitigate all perceived risks before the meeting. However, you are able to estimate the types of questions the different colleagues will ask. You can address them upfront and present your mitigating action.

By doing your homework before the qualification process, you will help your colleagues understand the importance of the opportunity. They will understand that you have put a lot of effort into it and want to take a serious look into the project's potential and see if it fits within the company's capacity.

Action: listen to your colleagues and sometimes agree with them.

Your colleagues have a lot of experience. During the qualification process, a lot of risks are identified. You should take note of them since you will need them for the rest of the commercial process. You do not need to mitigate all risks or solve all challenges during this stage, but it is good to be aware of them. You can use this information to educate your client.

Often your colleagues will have real objections and sometimes there is just too much risk in the project. In that case, you will need to follow their advice and disqualify the opportunity. Ask your colleagues what terms or in what way you could help your client instead. Keep the conversation constructive and challenge them on what is possible, rather than on what is not possible.

How the project execution factor fits in the whole process

The internal capacity to execute projects is the most common reason to disqualify an opportunity. The project execution factor is at the heart of internal discussions. It is the factor in which there are most interfaces with operational colleagues. If they do not like the opportunity, it is the workload that is often thrown in as an obstacle.

Sales does not always like the outcome of these discussions. Nevertheless, it is the capacity that will determine the amount of attention given to your project. The more attention the organization can give to an opportunity or a client, the better the perception of qualification will be. A happy client is one who will return. Unsatisfied clients will do more harm. In case the boundaries of the internal planning are stretched, you might end up making concessions on quality or timely performance, and this will affect the client's perceived value of it.

You can balance the project execution factor with the project potential. Some projects push the internal limits but might result in a lot of added value in the future. The next chapter covers this potential.

3.4 Project Potential's Impact

You are desperately trying to get your first opportunity with one of your Dream Clients. You are trying all the back doors to increase your chances. In the end, you promised yourself that you finally want to do business with this one client before the end of the year. You are on a mission and you are chasing this personal win.

In the heat of your daily battle, an email pops into your mailbox. A major Algerian contractor is requesting a call to discuss an opportunity to supply a specialized service to the state-owned oil major. The requested type of services are only used at well sites and since the end client operates many of them, the inquiry gets your attention. You decide to respond to the email.

During a phone call two days later, you find out more particulars of the opportunity. And your initial instinct was right. The business potential is huge.

You use the traditional BANT framework to qualify the lead. The budget seems to be available within the contractor and within the end client. You are able to verify that the request is genuine and you perform some basic due diligence. It seems that your contact person at the Algerian contractor is the right person with the right authority. This person explains clearly about the needs of the end client and what is in it for his company. On timing, the opportunity scores low. The lead time for the project is tight, but in normal circumstances, it would be feasible.

During an internal meeting, you present the opportunity to the attendants. You explain the opportunity, the parties involved, and your BANT evaluation. You thought that everyone in this meeting would be enthusiastic. However, this is not the case. Finance is worried about how to get money out of Algeria, operations point at their utilization factor of almost 100%, and engineering points to the slow review cycles of such clients.

Although you go into the meeting positively, you have a gut feeling that this scenario is realistic. Is there nobody who wants to win the jewels in the pipeline? Do project margin and big revenues not count anymore?

You cannot rely on the "Dream Client" or "Future A" concepts, since neither the end client nor the main contractor is on this list for obvious reasons. There is no leverage to pull out the urgency cart. You can also not count on a connection between this opportunity and the personal ambitions of your colleagues, and the organization's appetite seems far away from qualifying this opportunity.

The only argument that you have left is the business potential. What would this project mean to the company after a few years? What would be the spin-off? And, are there any opportunities to win (e.g. new technology, using old inventory, marketing potential)?

One thing is sure, you will need to convince your colleagues more before this opportunity will be qualified. You propose to postpone the qualification decision to next week. During that time, you will go through this chapter and prepare your case on the "business potential" argument.

> *Advice: work on storytelling to give your opportunity an extra edge.*

The ancient art of storytelling will boost qualification success. You are trying to create momentum to get your lucrative opportunity over the line. You really need to "sell" the opportunity internally. The best way to connect to people is by telling a story.

You can be as creative as you like. You can use past stories from within your company, or stories that resonate with your audience. You can even use stories from thriving species because they adapted to changing environments. Use whatever works to get your colleagues to understand the business potential of this opportunity.

> *Advice: paint the long-term picture.*

You should visualize the long-term positive and negative effects of winning the project. Finishing a project is often a moment of celebration or relief. These emotions can be triggered during the qualification meeting by visualizing how this might be.

Activate these feelings by visualizing the financial gains, the close-out meeting at your client's office, the feeling of accomplishment as a team. The most challenging projects are the most rewarding. These projects will go in the company's collective minds and those are the stories shared at parties.

You should differentiate between hard stats and the softer feelings of accomplishment so people don't think you're ridiculous.

> *Advice: show empathy for the situation you put your colleagues into.*

You understand that the decision to qualify the opportunity has a major impact on the business. You have to show that you care about the well-being of your colleagues. If you show empathy consistently, it is more likely your colleagues will try to put themselves in your shoes as well.

We are all human and we are operating in a larger setting. We all have our roles to play and have different responsibilities. For sales, it is bringing in new opportunities. Others are responsible for delivering. There will always be a conflict. Empathy is what should glue everything and everyone together.

> *Advice: search for connections between ambition and project potential.*

The ambition discussed in this chapter and the project potential often match up. If the project potential adds to the company's long-term goals, the opportunity will be qualified much faster. You will get support for the opportunity from within the organization.

> *Advice: use experience to estimate the total project value.*

In the complex environment we live in, projects never run as planned. Things change along the way, delays happen, or additional needs surface during the project. Experienced people within the company will be able to estimate the extent of extra financial gains of the project. You can also use a standard mark-up, which is the average of all past projects.

The risk of lost revenue, or extra work which is not paid, is working against qualification. The missing revenue or the risk of not being paid for additional services is a good reason to disqualify an opportunity.

At the tender phase, the tender team should estimate the total value and the margin of the complete project. This means that you will mark up (or decrease) the value by the extra expected gains (or losses). The full financial project potential should be the starting point of the qualification process.

Benefiting From the Project Potential in the Qualification Process

The project potential has a lot of similarities to other factors described in this book. The connection between the project and other company objectives (e.g. Dream Clients, ambition, etc.) make the qualification process such a challenge. That is the reason why standard frameworks often fall short.

The project potential should always be addressed during the qualification process.

Action: perform an ROI analysis on different output cases.

People like to see the immediate trade-off. It is easy to disqualify based on the direct returns of the project, but you have to look a few steps further down the line to see the indirect project potential.

For the Algerian opportunity, it would be the first step in the new market. The initial ROI of the project can already be positive. Adding the expanded project potential to the service, e.g. additional scope and after-service, the project becomes more profitable. When adding the opening of the new market, your ROI for the initial effort is even greater.

However, if the Algerian client is unwilling to pay for additional services or is not paying for parts of the initial scope, the total project value and margin should be adjusted. This will have an impact on the ROI and should be added as a worst-case scenario to the qualification briefing.

Action: create a storyboard of the journey during the project, at the end, and after the project.

Besides the figures presented in the previous action, you should visualize the project potential. Create a storyboard, which is self-explanatory. You can use humor to make the qualification process more fun and to address certain concerns or objections in a humorous way.

I would advise going all-in on creativity. The qualification meetings can be quite stressful because of mixed interests. By adding some disarming slides, you can relax the discussion. Of course, you need to stay professional, so try to find the right mix of static information and informal pictures.

Action: highlight the project potential in relation to other non-standard qualification factors.

There are many factors that influence the qualification process. The project potential will probably tap into a multitude of these factors. During the qualification process, you should highlight the parts of the project potential that are connected to other factors.

If the Algerian opportunity leads to increased business in a new target market and happened to be a long-term objective, then these two (project potential and market diversification) are a match. This match is valuable to senior management and the rest of the company. When you can show that the extraordinary project adds to the long-term goals of the company, people have the idea that they are heading in the right direction.

How Does the Project Potential Fit Into the Qualification Process?

If you draw a circle of the qualification process, the project potential would be the first circle around the traditional framework. The project potential factor is the most important group of factors influencing the qualification decision. It taps into the outer layers of the circles that have been described in the other sections of the book.

The project potential is the difference between the actual tender and future opportunities. It fills the gap that can be described as the indirect gains of the project. The indirect gains are not part of the direct returns of the project but can add value to the organization outside the standard scope. The additional scope can present opportunities to increase the indirect gains, but also allow entrance into new markets, start the first project with a Dream Client or Future A, or fit the corporate ambition.

The project potential is also what should influence the salespeople involved. They have to do a lot of additional work to land this challenging contract. They will need all the motivation they can find. The project potential has the potential to add motivation to salespeople. The personal pressures of the salespeople are the subject of the next chapter.

3.5 Summary

When we were transitioning from an engineering-only company to a turnkey contractor, it was great to be a salesperson. In fact, I was the first and only salesperson in the company. My added value to realize the company's ambitions was incredible. Every opportunity I brought in was cheered. The entire company was in full swing to make this transition work.

When we were growing rapidly, every project brought us closer to our goal. The industry was as positive as we were. We only had to raise our hand for opportunities and the requests were thrown at us. I just had to show a little bit of the project potential and the opportunity was qualified.

A few years down the line, things settled. The growth curve flattened, and the industry was suffering the effects of dropped oil prices. The years of growth took their toll. When everyone saw the future as paradise, it was easy to get people motivated. Now, the clouds were turning a little gray, and appetite for new business changed. The continuous flow of new opportunities slowed down and my colleagues were approaching the ones that came in with more pessimism.

The ambition changed from growth to continuity – continuity in terms of revenue, margin, but also in terms of keeping everyone on board. This change of ambition had a big impact on the qualification process.

The appetite had changed. The company worked under pressure for a long time. We had stretched the flexibility of the people in the company, and they were feeling a little tired. New opportunities were welcomed with a sigh of fatigue.

In terms of project execution, people were agreeable to perform the scope of work but were reluctant to give it their all. We had squeezed the resources too much for too long. The company was still performing well enough, but the great enthusiasm was temporarily gone.

Our clients were spending less money and were more hesitant to invest in our types of services. The requests for quotations and tenders reflected this trend. We had to search hard for the project's potential to extend beyond the immediate financial returns.

This example shows that the qualification process is affected by the internal pressures described in this chapter. Each day, the qualification process can be different. It depends on the vibes within your organization and the feeling of the individual employees. This feeling of the employees will be the subject of the next chapter.

In Chapter 2, we dealt with the external pressures, which play an important role in the qualification process. The impacting factors connect to the internal pressures. Internally, some additional factors are added to the qualification play. These internal pressures are outlined in this chapter.

The next chapter will zoom in further into the individual level. The influence of people within your company should not be underestimated and, therefore, this topic deserves a complete chapter.

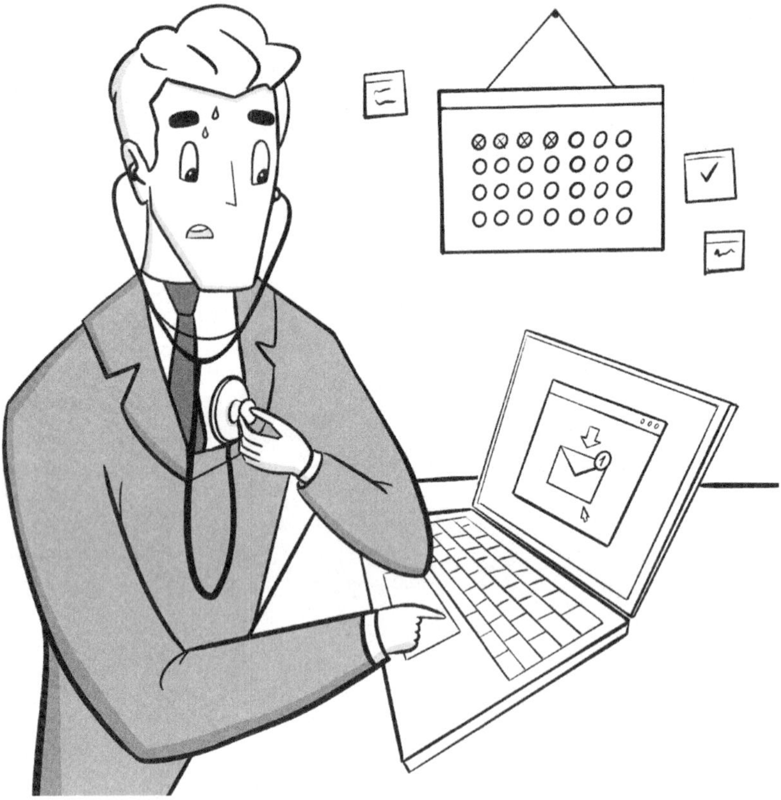

Personal Pressures

There are four emotional stages in the qualification process.

- Strong initial feeling
- Contra-feelings
- Justification and rationalization
- Acceptance

The concept of the emotional stages is part of the reason companies introduce a qualification framework. They try to eliminate the subjective personal factors that influence the decision-making process. The personal feeling of one individual should not have an impact on the business.

In real life, it is humans that are making decisions. The qualification process can only be done by people. Computers only have a supportive role. This might seem a conservative approach, however, it is also humans who have to execute most of the project in the event it is won. As such, you better involve real people in the qualification process. Otherwise, it is unlikely that the organization will stay motivated to make the best out of the project.

Like the previous exceptions presented in this book, personal influence greatly affects the qualification process. Before the major personal factors are outlined, the four emotional stages are explained in more detail.

Four emotional stages in the qualification process
We experience the world differently. Challenges presented follow a similar path, from an impactful start to an easy final feeling. The qualification process is no different. By recognizing the different

stages, the qualification process will not feel like a rollercoaster of feelings.

Strong initial feeling

The first emotional phase starts when the new opportunity reaches your mailbox or when a client expresses a need for your service. You have been working hard to get to this level. The opportunity is a major milestone in your commercial process. Once the opportunity is clear, you will feel a sense of accomplishment.

The first glimpse of the new request is followed by a strong initial feeling. When the opportunity looks good, you will feel really excited. It will feel like you have already won the project.

When the opportunity is not in line with what you tried to sell, you will feel very disappointed. You know you have to start over with the commercial process or try to convince the rest of the organization that this opportunity is still worthwhile. You feel disappointed because you were unable to explain what you can offer.

You share this strong feeling with your direct colleagues and your manager. You let it sink in for a bit of time and you receive some initial feedback from your colleagues before you enter the next phase.

Contra-feeling

After a day or two, you have created so many objections in your head that your initial feeling is contradicted. In case of a negative initial feeling, you have created so many opportunities that you feel the rest of the organization will buy into your story and qualify the opportunity.

During this stage, you have contradictory feelings from the initial phase. The emotional peak is not as high as the initial feeling, rather it contradicts it. This might make you insecure. However, it is a vital stage in opportunity qualification.

During the contra-feeling stage, you are gathering your thoughts to go into the next phase. The experiences are often subconscious. The feelings try to prepare you for an undesired outcome.

This phase separates the qualification process from the outcome. Therefore, it is an essential part of your personal quest. This phase costs a significant amount of energy since you experience mixed feelings.

Justification and rationalization

This phase is marked by initial acceptance of reality. All the pros and cons are gathered to make a justified qualification decision. The contra-feeling phase is completed by starting the rationalization process. All your thoughts and feelings are put into perspective and start to make sense.

It is the summary that you bring into the qualification decision. You understand the rationales behind the opportunity and have made up your mind. You create the battle plan to either convince the rest of the organization, let the rest of the organization decide, or tell the client your intention to decline.

When moving to the next phase, it will be easier for you to understand the group decision.

Acceptance

The stage of acceptance is where the qualification decision is made. The resulting actions are outlined, and the qualification process is concluded. You have to accept the group decision, which is often in line with your preferred outcome.

The initial feeling when the opportunity was presented has changed. The outcome of the qualification process might be different from initially expected, but our emotional stages have guided you to accept the qualification process outcome. You have tried to influence the decision and, probably, you succeeded. You now have to bear the consequences.

Opportunity qualification is a process. Be patient and compassionate with yourself. You're not alone.

This chapter will explain how to use timing, fear, and excitement when qualifying opportunities. These factors are subject to how we experience the process and at what emotional stage we are in. Salespeople are required to juggle all balls to get the outcome they desire and hope it is aligned with the corporate strategy and ambition.

4.1 Personal Timing

All salespeople know it. They can act as gatekeepers for certain opportunities. If they feel excited, they will use all their creativity to let the qualification process have a positive outcome. The other way around is true as well. Not only salespeople can influence based on personal criteria, but this power also lies with many more in the organization. Understanding these personal pressures will improve the qualification process.

Timing is key. Do the salespeople have a full pipeline or do they need to add opportunities? If the holiday period arrives, then the personal appetite might be less. And what about the mood of the day or the recent experiences of individuals?

When I am writing the first version of this chapter, I feel super and full of energy. If a Future A client called me right now, I would jump into the opportunity with everything I have got. I have plenty of time to make the first proposal before my holiday starts. My pipeline is doing OK. I would welcome this opportunity. If I were not writing this book now, I would get on the phone to see if there was an opportunity into which I could put all my energy.

Last week was different. The weekend was full of social gatherings and my little boy kept me up at night. With limited sleep, I stared at my screen. Two opportunities were in my inbox. One was a straightforward job on the North Sea, one of a dozen. And, one was an off-the-beaten-track opportunity. I could only disqualify the latter one, which I did. I was lucky enough that I could delegate the standard opportunity. I was just not motivated to attack both.

> *Advice: recognize your mood and that of the people around you.*

Sales requires proactive behavior and commitment. There is not one person that hasn't experienced peaks and valleys in their mood. These changes often have personal roots. Salespeople have to act like a psychiatrist to recognize their own moods and those of the people around them.

When you are in a pessimistic mood and you feel this day is worthless, admit it to yourself. If extraordinary requests reach your mailbox on such a day, allow yourself a day extra to react, or forward the request to a colleague or your manager to receive their opinion. Above all, understand that your emotional state might make you reluctant to accept new adventures and that it influences your decisions.

If you see a colleague with a heavy workload or you find out that there is a flaw in his private life, reach out and ask what is on his plate. If you see them struggling to take on new opportunities that require a lot of energy, offer to take over the opportunity or just lend a helping hand. Sales is not a game you play individually. It is the responsibility of the entire team and maybe of the entire company. It should not depend on the mental status of one individual.

> *Advice: track holiday planning and mitigate the inappropriate disqualification risk.*

There is a chance that salespeople will influence the qualification negatively just before their holiday starts. Salespeople know that at the beginning of each commercial process and two weeks after submission of the first proposal, a lot of communication is needed. Besides that, there are administrative duties and there is the pressure to clean their desks. In the end, some salespeople are really committed to freeing their holiday from any work-related activity.

We might not accept it, but we should understand that this is happening. Maybe we should even support this kind of behavior to allow the salesperson quality time off. By making this topic discussable, you will create an open environment in which this can be discussed. Managers send a message that they care about the team by allowing them to have work-free holidays.

Managers of sales teams should promote a qualification grace period for salespeople. For example, three weeks before salespeople's annual holiday starts, they should start handing over opportunities to their colleagues before disqualifications. This might feel counterintuitive, but your company's opportunity pipeline will benefit.

> *Advice: monitor individual sales pipelines.*

There is a direct correlation between the individual sales pipeline of salespeople and the types of opportunities they are qualifying.

With an overly full pipeline, salespeople might only qualify for opportunities that are easy to win. Or, when they still have plenty of space on their agenda, they might accept an additional challenging project to keep them from boredom.

Salespeople in need of additional projects in their pipelines will accept close to anything to show that their work pays off. This behavior is toxic because you start chasing ghost projects as an organization. It also allows salespeople to slow down prospecting.

Companies have to understand that salespeople are operating under pressure. They have the natural desire to show a full pipeline. The quality of the pipeline is not the priority for many salespeople; they only want to show that their efforts pay off. Full individual pipelines might cause disqualification, however, the organization might have benefited from this opportunity and lost out.

> *Advice: use the mental peaks.*

There are always members of the sales team who are going really strongly. It seems that they can conquer the world and that they are ready to pick up any fight. You can introduce them to the qualification process. They will shine a positive light on the opportunity and all stakeholders will be enthused.

The positive person should get an active role in the qualification process and in winning the deal. In this state of mind, it is these salespeople who are on a path to success. This might be temporary but use this energy to get the opportunities presented when they are at their peaks.

How to benefit from personal timing in the qualification process

The impact of individual mental states of salespeople on the disqualification is a risk or an opportunity in the qualification process. The timing of opportunities is, therefore, a big factor that influences the decision process. There are many ways to mitigate the risk of timing and to seize the opportunity presented because of timing.

Action: disconnect the personal pipelines from the qualification process.

Create an environment in which all new opportunities are entered into a CRM system. Even opportunities that are obviously out of scope. By monitoring the incoming opportunities, the organization can steer in the right direction. Salespeople can be asked for their initial qualification decision.

The sales team can act as one and find the right team member to attack the right opportunity. With tracking in CRM, you create an environment of accountability. It will flatten peaks with one team member because others will take over (parts of) their work.

How can you disconnect the personal pipeline from the qualification process? This has to be embedded in the company or team culture. You have to start acting as one team. Make the team accountable for the team result and make the personal targets of less importance.

Action: introduce a grace period before the holiday.

If I am honest, I have declined opportunities in the past that were presented within the last few weeks before my holiday. I know that when accepting the opportunity, I would need to stress to get the bid out before my holiday. I could use this time to close files and to make sure that all other opportunities were followed up appropriately.

I was motivated to grant myself a work-free holiday, which means receiving a limited number of phone calls and a limited number of urgent emails.

When I became a manager, I embraced this concept for my team members. I encouraged them to clear their agendas before their holidays. This was not only to allow them quality time but also to keep up the quality of the commercial process. I know that when clients call a person who is on holiday, they might not be served well.

A grace period, e.g. a couple of weeks before the holiday, offers time to prepare for the holiday. During this grace period, salespeople are encouraged not to take on big commercial projects. They are encouraged to hand over opportunities at an early stage to one of their colleagues.

Some salespeople find it hard to hand over control of their prospects. It is the manager who should explain the reasons why: the holiday is a time to relax and to experience quality time and the prospect deserves someone who is fully committed to delivering great support. In the beginning, this might feel strange to the team, but after a while, they will feel the positive effects.

How does personal timing fit into the qualification process?

We have been discussing all kinds of factors influencing the qualification process. Often these factors are exceptions to the standard qualification frameworks. These exceptions, such as Dream Clients, Future A, urgent opportunities, etc., will cost additional effort for salespeople.

Salespeople require additional motivation to convince their colleagues that the opportunity is qualified. They will also have more challenges to win the contract. If you task your sales team to hunt for standard opportunities, then these opportunities can be considered extracurricular. These kinds of opportunities require energy and attention.

In this section, we have seen the impact of emotional state, upcoming holiday periods, and the effect of the individual pipeline on the qualification process. If the opportunity was presented at another time, the outcome of the qualification process might have been different.

Besides timing, there is also the fear of missing out and personal excitement that affects the qualification process. These personal pressures will be discussed next.

4.2 Personal Fear

A new opportunity kept Michael awake at night. He was asked to provide an extensive scope of work for one of his Dream Clients at a remote site in Papua New Guinea. The base scope included the supply of a water management system. The extended scope (removing the old system) and the location made him doubt the opportunity.

In bed, he went over all the qualification criteria. He spent months getting to this point with this Dream Client. He traveled to their headquarters in Paris regularly to meet with many people within the company. The target people were all positive about Michael's offer, but it had not resulted in an inquiry yet.

Michael felt the pressure of his pipeline drying up. There were no big deals on the horizon and his employment contract was nearing its end.

Michael finally got the chance to bring in business from this promising account. Since it would be the company's first time working with this client, the startup of the project could prove to be challenging. Both Michael's team in the UK and the US had to start collaborating with the client's team in France. Michael was a little pessimistic about the outcome of this cooperation.

Michael found himself torn between qualification and disqualification. He had a fear of missing out on a very nice deal. He worried about making a bad decision. Although he did not need to make the qualification decision on his own, the outcome would depend on how he started the internal process.

It is typically the company culture and the internal processes that dictate the amount of fear that salespeople experience during the qualification process. Michael's situation is not an exception. These are the kind of pressures that salespeople have to deal with. For salespeople who are already established within their company, the fear might move more externally: "Can the organization meet the expectations of the client?" But there is always fear resulting in personal pressures.

> *Advice: discuss opportunities with peers.*

A great way to structure your thoughts is to discuss new opportunities with peers. This naturally happens when you are in the same office, but you should not underestimate the power of doing so in other settings as well. More and more salespeople are working remotely, which might fuel their anxiety. Peer-to-peer conversations will help to ease the qualification process.

An informal setting in which people can feel safe needs to be established to discuss all kinds of personal struggles amongst peers. The relationship between peers should be based on trust and on constructive advice. When there are personal struggles within the team, the atmosphere will hamper the decision process. In a non-constructive environment, salespeople will keep the opportunities to themselves, which might make good qualification decisions difficult.

> *Advice: recognize the fears within the sales team.*

A lot of western cultures dictate that fear is a sign of weakness. It probably finds its origin in nature, where weak creatures are the first to be attacked. Within corporate structures fear might also be a sign of weaknesses, which might be perceived as being a risk to the personal position of a salesperson. Therefore, it can be hard to recognize fear.

Fear during the qualification process is not prominent since it is not jeopardizing our lives. This makes it even harder to recognize.

You can find out about fears during the qualification process by staying closely connected. Ask the right questions and see how the salesperson reacts. When they express negativity towards an opportunity, you should question their judgment. They might be in fear of making the wrong decision and they want you to convince them that the opportunity should be qualified. When you are trying to convince them, they feel supported and see that you are committed to the opportunity.

If you feel that the salesperson is over-optimistic, it might be a sign of fear of missing out. Look at their project pipeline and their position in the company for clues on the 'fear of missing out'.

In both fear cases, there probably will be a delay in the qualification process. The opportunity might be sitting in the inbox of the salesperson for a few days. The salesperson only presents it during your scheduled next meeting. If there was no fear in play, they would probably have reported the opportunity before the meeting.

> *Advice: empathy is your best friend.*

Modern leadership is about vision and empathy. Empathic leaders will accompany their colleagues along the journey. They will stand alongside and back up their colleagues. Empathy is the grease you need during the qualification process.

"Why do you always bring in these kinds of opportunities" or "Don't waste the organization's time with this", are examples of statements that kill the qualification process. These remarks will fuel the feeling of fear. They close the doors for future non-standard opportunities.

If you want your company only to work on opportunities that fit the standard qualification framework, and you do not want your sales team to challenge the system, you do not need to show empathy. But you are reading this book, so you understand the power of entrepreneurship. Empathy will bring you entrepreneurial behavior within your sales team. People allow creativity into their work when there is no fear of the leadership being stubborn or critical.

How to Benefit From Fear During the Qualification Process

We teach salespeople that people buy emotionally and justify rationally. You are trying to move your prospect in an emotional stage so they will act. You are trying to solve a pressing need to make their future better.

The same is true for your sales team. When they get emotionally connected to an opportunity, the chances of success are much higher. Fear in itself is counterproductive but can be changed easily to excitement. Fear is an emotional state we naturally try to avoid. When dealt with appropriately, fear can be changed to our benefit easily.

Action: initiate peer-to-peer meetings and put qualification on the agenda.

Especially when the members of the sales team are not in the same office, it is up to the manager to accommodate meetings amongst direct colleagues. Colleagues can learn a lot from each other and sometimes need a mirror. The collective brainpower of colleagues will result in more creative ways of approaching clients and decisions.

The agenda should be set by the meeting attendants. However, sales management can provide suggestions to put the open opportunities on the agenda. For new opportunities, the qualification will be part of the discussion. For more mature opportunities, the peers will automatically discuss how to increase the chances of winning. The meeting will also provide space to complain about internal matters, which is a valuable topic to discuss amongst peers.

For all the sales teams I have worked with, I have implemented peer-to-peer meetings. They are very effective and take some pressure off the agendas of sales leaders. Part of the coaching is organized amongst peers. Salespeople tend to get a lot of (creative) energy from these meetings, which has broader results than only contributing to the qualification process.

Action: actively put fear to rest.

Since we now understand the concept of fear, we are able to change the mental state of salespeople. When addressing the fear that your salespeople may have, they feel recognized. You create an environment in which fears (and other emotions) can be discussed. This environment is very fruitful and needs to be nurtured at all times.

After recognizing the fear, put these fears to rest. Support the salesperson by personally committing to the qualification process and the outcome of the further commercial process. Give the notion that you are in it together without taking over the opportunity. If the project is won, the salesperson can take the credit. If the project is lost, it is a joint failure.

Action: create awareness within the rest of the organization.

During the qualification process, other departments will join the discussion. They have a different agenda from the sales team. They have a fear that they cannot deliver what is being promised by the sales team. This fear is different from the "fear of missing out" or the "fear of making a wrong decision".

By creating awareness of the sales fears, the rest of the organization understands where you are coming from. If, for example, the pipeline is drying up, this fear should be addressed during the qualification meeting. The personal pipeline can be part of the same discussion. Colleagues will understand that salespeople will put in a lot of effort to bring the opportunity over the finish line when they have an empty pipeline. They understand the salespeople's motives and can use this to their advantage.

How Does Personal Fear Fit into the Qualification Process?

I started off this chapter with the example of Michael chasing an opportunity in Papua New Guinea. We understood his dilemma. When he woke up in the morning, he knew what to do. He talked to one of his colleagues about the opportunity, who then guided him in the direction of the construction manager. During Michael's discussion with the construction manager, he soon found out that qualification might be difficult due to financial risks.

Michael had not seen this risk but decided to involve the finance manager in the discussion. The finance manager did not perceive this risk. After several other discussions, Michael became more and more excited and felt comfortable about the opportunity. He started the qualification process and the team decided to quote for the complete project.

Michael turned his fear into motivation. He was committed to winning the project and securing entrance into the new Dream Client. When Michael returned home one night, he told his wife that he was onto this new opportunity. He was talking with so much excitement that his wife was confused, "Isn't that the same opportunity that kept you awake last week?"

We are in a world where rational decisions are the norm, but there is a human aspect to decision making. In the previous paragraphs, the timing was discussed. The timing of an opportunity will influence the outcome of the qualification process. If it does not fit into the salesperson's plan, the opportunity might be disqualified. Fear adds another layer to the level of personal influence on opportunities.

In the next section, I will dive into "excitement" and how the qualification process can benefit. It is the glue that keeps the organization together. There is no need to show up at work if there is no excitement.

4.3 Personal Excitement

There is one thing nicer than getting a new opportunity in a new targeted market. That is, when one of your team gets this opportunity. It is great to see the excitement in people who have worked hard to realize this next step, especially if you were part of their journey as mentor or coach. The salesperson runs into your office like a child who managed to ride a bike for the first time.

Excitement easily transforms into motivation to win the tender. The excitement of this one person is infectious and has a positive impact on the rest of the organization.

When Paul called me during his business trip to the US, he was so excited that people were staring at him. If the police had stopped by, they might well have arrested him for being on some kind of drug. He kept stumbling over his words to tell me about the opportunity that was so hot, he could barely believe it. I heard a sigh of relief in his voice. A touch of self-recognition confirming he was a good salesperson.

I understood his excitement. Paul sold his SME company, and the new owner kept him on in the business. Paul had sold the company with a story that expansion was possible. He had promised new markets would open once there was a larger financial backing. In the nine-month period, Paul focused on getting new business in the US, where he never did business before the take-over. The feeling within the company was that the US was too hard to enter due to government restrictions (unions, visas, etc.). But Paul was stubborn, and wanted to succeed.

Paul was the owner and managing director of the company before it was sold. He grew the company from five to 50 people. He had a small sales team who reported to him. Paul always had the impression that he could do better than his sales team. I was the first salesperson within his company. When the company was taken over, I moved to the sales team management position and Paul was officially part of my team.

We can all relate to Paul's excitement. His case was, of course, unique, but we have all had moments in our lives when we were so happy about a new opportunity. Those opportunities often happen at exactly the right time in your personal life. Sometimes, you may even want to give up and then all of a sudden, this great opportunity pops up.

> *Advice: keep the excitement as long as you can*

When Paul hung up the phone to cool down, he started reaching out to others within the organization to tell them about this new opportunity. It is logical for others to try to beat the excitement down. Paul's operational colleagues explained all the risks and challenges involved.

After the second phone call, Paul lost part of his excitement.

This is a true loss of energy. Paul should have celebrated the new opportunity himself for a bit longer. He could have waited before calling his colleagues in the morning. Paul would have already been at ease with the new opportunity and could have put his excitement to the side to revel in it at a later stage.

Many parts of the commercial process require this excitement. You should figure out a way to control the excitement and to use it to your advantage. When you start letting yourself be beaten down when you are at your excitement peak, it will be hard to get back to this "little space" where you can recharge your previous excitement.

> *Advice: use excitement to convince and facts to support.*

During the qualification process, excitement can have two results. One is that other people will join the excitement or, alternatively, it might cause people to be careful. Excited salespeople are often thought to be opportunists. They are regarded as over-optimistic and having no eye on the project's challenges. Excited salespeople only think of the lucrative contract and forget about the consequences during the project execution.

Salespeople should use their excitement to balance the observed challenges. Salespeople show the risks that they have identified and indicate the direction of mitigation. They can use their excitement to fuel the pursuit of risk mitigation. Salespeople are not the ones required to mitigate most of the risks, but they will need to motivate their colleagues to do the hard work.

> *Advice: spread your excitement during the qualification process.*

During the qualification process, operational colleagues are typically transitioning from pessimistic to a more positive mindset. They will use the final decision and your excitement to motivate themselves to execute their roles.

Besides the rationality of the qualification process, there is a big portion of emotions involved. Emotions can sometimes work counterproductively, or they can increase motivation. At least, when there are emotions in play, things start to move. If you are able to get the rest of the organization on your train of excitement, the train will keep moving fast.

Benefiting from excitement in the qualification process
It seems the easiest thing to benefit from excitement during the tender process. However, there is also a risk that you will take the opportunity too lightly. You might overlook risks to a successful tender. You might miss the number of details you are required to provide and run into deadline issues. You might miss competitors entering the scene. You might miss changes in the prospect's decision-making unit.

Action: keep an eye on the target.

During the qualification process, excitement will push your opportunity over the line internally. People will join in having enthusiasm for the project. Your colleagues will feel that the tender process will be a walk in the park, but you need to stay focused.

Work your normal process, as if the opportunity is one that requires a battle. Your team has to work out all the details and stay on top of their commercial game. The initial excitement is not a ticket to winning the contract. A lot needs to happen until the signature is obtained.

Action: journal the opportunities that cause excitement.

Journaling is one of the best ways to track emotions and to learn from them. In the case of excitement during the initial phases of a tender, it is especially true. The tender process will provide you with challenges: objections from colleagues, tender deadlines, technical obstacles, etc. If you read back in your journal about your excitement at the start of the tender, you might rediscover the motivation.

With journaling, you might also identify trends in your feelings. When you understand these trends, you are more likely to replicate them.

You can also use this excitement to give your bid submission an extra flavor. This personal story will show your client that there are real people working with their supplier. It will make the business transaction more human. The negotiation phase and the project execution will benefit from this.

How Excitement Fits Into the Qualification Process

In the previous section, fear was addressed. The fear of missing out or the fear of making a wrong decision are emotions that affect the decision-making process. By contrast, there are a lot of positive emotions that influence decisions. If only fear was the emotion to make the qualification decision, not a lot of business opportunities would be qualified.

Within every organization, excitement for new opportunities needs to be present. It is this excitement that makes people work within your organization. If the projects in your pipeline are not exciting for the majority of your company, your company would not exist.

Bringing this excitement into the qualification process is logical. Traditional qualification frameworks try to ignore personal excitement; however, this can be a very good driver to continue with the opportunity. If the opportunity is not perfect as per BANT, MEDDICC or one of the other frameworks, it might be the excitement of individuals that makes the difference in the qualification process.

It is the excitement that makes people go the extra mile. It is the excitement that induces people to get out of bed in the morning.

4.4 New-Colleagues

After numerous attempts to grow the business in Indonesia, we decided to invest in people on the ground. Indonesia offers a vibrant industrial market, in which it is hard to penetrate as a foreign entity. The local practices are tough to understand. It seems that you have to be born in Indonesia to really get a grasp of business acumen.

We decided to hire a young local person to cover that market. During our quest to find the right person, we learned that there is a great variety of commercial professionals: those who have an established network and are asking for significant salaries, and junior people who are at the start of their careers. We decided that the second group would work for us and selected someone with good English skills, and who was flexible and smart.

After 18 months, no new business came in from the market. This was in line with expectations; however, the local rep advised us to hire a local agent with whom to partner. His main point was that a local agent has more room to play and an existing network. Consequently, we contracted a local agent as a partner.

Soon the first inquiries began coming in. Both our local rep and the local agent were pleased that these RFQs were delivered to our company. To them, it proved that this setup would be successful.

In HQ, they thought differently. They were openly questioning the quality of the opportunities presented. Operational teams were questioning the project fit and the management team doubted that we could be cost-competitive. Do we need to invest time in preparing the proposals? What is going on with this market?

We felt the pressure of the ambition of the local rep and agent. They were feeling motivated to bring business and were happy that things were moving. If we disqualified these first opportunities their motivation might drop. The local team believed in the quality of the opportunities and felt that the Indonesian market was different. They really had the feeling that they could win the projects and wanted to receive a quote from HQ.

> *Advice: save the first opportunities and qualify at least half.*

In the above case, HQ should not disqualify all opportunities. They should explain the reasons for their doubts. They should make the local rep and agent part of their thinking process. The doubts HQ have can be a good lesson to the Indonesian team. Of course, the local team will question HQ's concerns. They will feel that they have the local knowledge and that their commercial senses are right.

By qualifying some of the opportunities and providing the required input to return to the new prospects, the local team can learn and maybe you will be surprised by what the local team can accomplish. If it does not result in business, you will benefit from the learning experience. The local team will be targeting more effectively in the future.

> *Advice: understand the correlation between disqualification and motivation.*

A motivated team is worth more than your current projects. A motivated team pushes the boundaries to grow. If you have new people on your team, it is most important to keep motivating them. If you hammer their motivation in their first few months on the job, you might lose potentially good salespeople. You have to invest time in them.

Maybe you still remember when you first entered the sales arena. You were ambitious and anxious. It takes a lot of time to land your first opportunity. Once you received the inquiry in your mailbox, you were beyond ecstatic and could not wait to tell the people around you. The reaction of your colleagues will make or break your motivation. By receiving the first opportunities, you were climbing out of a state of insecurity. People around you had the chance to knock you back. But, by praising your new opportunity and celebrating the success together, you left the dark space of insecurity for good.

> *Advice: let new people target broadly in the beginning.*

If you keep the commercial efforts of new team members focused on the most qualified opportunities, they will have difficulties getting their first opportunities. It is hard to find a needle in a haystack. It requires a lot of time and effort to find one. The motivation of your new colleague will be put too much to the test.

It might make sense to educate newbies from day one. You might want to make them razor sharp. But in my experience, this is too big of a burden.

Provide the new salespeople with a broader range of services. Let them investigate the best ways into the prospect's organization. They will learn more from less qualified opportunities than having to wait for the perfect fit. You will get more motivated salespeople in return.

Benefiting From New Colleagues in the Qualification Process

New people will bring new experiences and a fresh take on the market. We all understand that the energy of the new person can work like an oil spill onto the rest of the team. We should allow this energy to flow freely and for as long as possible. The qualification process can benefit from the new person on the team. You might consider qualifying from the new person an opportunity that would most likely have been disqualified when brought into your funnel by an experienced salesperson.

Action: create qualification categories.

On the first day that your new colleagues or new external business partners (distributors or agents) join your team, you will start to educate them on your service portfolio. You will start with the most common services you provide, and which clients buy those services. Soon, you will run into more complex projects, and after a while, you will present the projects which were not so nice to deal with.

In every business, there are services that are very rewarding and services that are not so favorable. It is important to understand what the different categories are and why certain opportunities are more favorable than others. The reasons are often the qualification criteria outlined in this book: the amount of competition, the complexity of the project, and the nature of the client.

Creating an overview of the different types of opportunities in terms of the qualification process is a good way to visualize the potential market. The new person can work their way through the categories and find the balance in their prospecting efforts.

Suitable categories can be: preferred opportunities (highly qualified), special projects (medium qualified), filling-up work (low qualified), and off-grid (unqualified).

The last category is important. Everyone in the organization knows what opportunities will be presented to the new person that is "off-grid". Clients have been asking for this service for many years and the opportunities are like wolves in disguise. The project is presented as a really good opportunity and might excite the new salesperson, but the whole organization already knows it is up for disqualification. From the start, It is better to educate the new salesperson to prevent running into that trap.

Action: use the new person to motivate the organization.

The new person will be positive towards the market. They will probably believe that their new employer is the best in the field. The new person will be running through their first qualification processes with great enthusiasm and this enthusiasm is contagious. The whole organization will benefit from the energy brought by the new person.

Action: regard qualification as an onboarding investment.

Onboarding new salespeople, agents, or distributors costs time and effort. We have to set aside time and resources to train them. It is

OK to spend a lot of time transferring knowledge. But they learn best when they experience situations themselves.

The best experience you can get is in front of prospects and clients. To run a full commercial process with the client, the new person needs input from HQ. This will include significant homework to be done by HQ. By disqualifying a large number of the opportunities presented by the new person, the learning curve will be longer.

Consider making time available to work on opportunities that would normally be disqualified. Use these opportunities to train the new people on the job. These experiences will be much more settled in the brain of the new person than presenting theoretical cases via a slide show.

How Does the New Person fit in the Qualification Process?

New people within your commercial organization have the potential to add a lot of value. They will bring energy and new insights. They will create opportunities with different prospects and from a slightly different angle. The immediate gains of new people cannot be underestimated.

Most of the initial gains will be the result of the energy that is present when people begin to attack a new challenge. This energy will be transferred to the rest of the team and the organization. Or it can be hammered down within the first weeks of having the new person on board.

For commercial people, the most demotivation is the result of disqualified opportunities. Salespeople are fine when they lose to competition, but they feel really bad if they feel unsupported by their organization. When salespeople feel they have a good opportunity and the rest of the organization is blocking the commercial process, it will have a direct impact on their motivation.

For new people, this factor cannot be underestimated. You can destroy the energy of new people easily when saying no to their hard-fought opportunities. If you do that often enough, you will soon have a demotivated salesperson on your team. It will take a lot of time to get this person out of this downward spiral.

In this section, you have learned that the qualification of opportunities brought by new people is different from those brought by experienced people. It correlates with the other emotional states discussed in this chapter, like excitement and fear. And it is closely connected to the timing as discussed in the first section of this chapter.

4.5 Summary

"Ignorance is the parent of fear" is a famous 19th-century quote from Herman Melville, the writer of *Moby Dick*. When we are chasing opportunities the way Ahab chased Moby Dick (the whale), we might get hurt. It is our resilience that keeps us going. We do not need to hide from the personal pressures that play upon us in chasing our whales.

In this chapter, we have learned that personal feelings, like fear and excitement, influence the qualification process. And that timing makes us act differently in comparable situations. We should not be ignorant of these facts. When embracing the pressures, we need to recognize them and act upon them.

Traditional qualification frameworks ignore personal pressures. They try to rationalize the qualification process. However, the traditional models will fall short because the input is manipulated by humans.

Salespeople are manipulating the input to get their favorite output of the qualification process. They will use everything in their power, e.g. Dream Clients, the organization's appetite, and/or resource planning, to convince the rest of the organization to qualify or disqualify. These attempts are fueled by what is happening in their minds.

Previously in this chapter the concept of "timing" was discussed. Interesting opportunities today might look less interesting tomorrow. The moment the opportunity presents itself determines the outcome of the qualification process. By recognizing the effect of the personal planning of the decision makers, it can become part of the discussion: "Would we have accepted the opportunity one year ago or next year?"

Personal feelings like fear and excitement can both work in two directions. It can stimulate qualification as well as disqualification. These individual feelings might overshadow a proper qualification decision, but they can also be used to the advantage of the process.

It is exactly these emotions that can make the difference in dealing with the tender pressures, which is the topic of the next chapter. The motivation to participate in the tender has been discussed in this and the previous two chapters. The tender pressures can also be a reason for disqualification or qualification. The more pressures, the more resources, and the more risks are involved.

Tender Pressures

In my attic, I still hold a copy of Sun Tzu's *Art of War*. One passage strikes me when I think of the tender pressures. "There are five essentials for victory: He will win who knows when to fight and when not to fight. He will win who knows how to handle both superior and inferior forces. He will win whose army is animated by the same spirit throughout all its ranks. He will win who prepared himself, waits to take the enemy unprepared. He will win who has military capacity and is not interfered with by the sovereign."

This wisdom finds its origins in the 5th century BCE and is still true today. You have to pick your battles and overcome obstacles together with like-minded people around you. The tendering process is not a fight over life. However, it is one with many obstacles which you cannot overcome individually.

This chapter is devoted to the pressures that directly come from the tender. There are many links to other parts of the book and references will be made to standard qualification frameworks. After completing this chapter, you will have completed the qualification process and you can call yourself a true professional.

I will start by describing the pressures resulting from the tender process and the different stages will be discussed, which are: pre-RFQ, initial qualification, approaching deadline. In all these stages, there is a direct connection with the qualification process.

Your subcontractors and others in the supply chain influence your tender as well. In the first phases of the tender process, you might have established partnerships that bring mutual expectations. These expectations will influence the tender and qualification process.

Many salespeople dislike tender processes because of the level of detail. Besides the scope of work, the tender package includes terms and conditions, Quality, Health, Safety & Environment (QHSE) requirements, financial forms, and the list continues. All these specifications are pressing on the qualification process. The specifications will be discussed in section 5.4.

You will learn how to re-cap the lessons and conclude if the project fits your organization. If all signs are green, you still might want to consider if the project is a good fit. Even at this very last resort, you might want to consider qualification or disqualification. The project fit is the subject of the last paragraph of this chapter.

5.1 Tender Process

My team was chasing a bridge construction project in the South of Spain. The pre-qualification process was completed almost two years prior. We had to submit a lot of documents, forms, and evidence to get ourselves pre-qualified. Although we almost gave up, we managed to pre-qualify.

Our sales rep Juan had followed up with the client periodically. He would call or email once every month to find out about the status of the project. The message was the same every month: "We are awaiting final approval from the government, and then we kick off immediately. We expect the next step by next month." In March 2022, Juan resigned and joined one of our competitors.

Five weeks after Juan's resignation, we received the official tender documents. The new sales rep for the region downloaded all the documents to store them on our servers. IT noticed a red flag appearing when uploading the 8 GB of data. Luckily, the data seemed quite well organized at first glance. We went through the folders to pull out the scope of work, which was a clearly written document. There were not too many references to other documents, which made it easy to read.

The next day, the sales rep acknowledged receipt and our intention to bid. He then planned a qualification meeting for five days later, allowing everyone sufficient time to screen the tender. He invited an experienced project manager, the manager of operations, and the manager of the sales team. This group of four should be able to make a solid qualification call.

Before the meeting, the sales rep tried to get a clear understanding of the complete project. He wanted to influence his constituency before the qualification meeting. He tried to motivate his legal colleague to make an initial assessment of the terms and conditions and tried to get the QHSE requirements under the attention of the QHSE department.

All is good so far. While working on the last significant tender, the sales rep received feedback that he was not prepared well enough to get the best out of the tender process. This time, the sales rep was determined to do better.

> *Advice: always be prepared to escalate.*

Tenders do not drop in your mailbox when you have nothing else on your plate. They drop in at the worst possible times with deadlines that do not meet your free space in your agenda. You should be prepared for tenders to drop in at any time. You need to understand how to escalate and start the process without having to run through the complete tender package and having to ask your manager.

You should be able to forward the required documents to the different stakeholders. You should plan a meeting internally and you should acknowledge receipt. All of these activities should be completed within one hour.

> *Advice: manage expectations from the start of the qualification process.*

The tender process is one of managing expectations. You can manage expectations by clearly communicating the tender process milestones. You should immediately outline to your colleagues when you will be performing the initial qualification and when the tender submission deadline is.

Let the key stakeholders within your organization know at what point you will need their opinion and input. If you involve them one day prior to the decision, you might create an undesired situation. If you forgot to involve people early in the process, communicate clearly that their opinion is really appreciated and apologize for involving them late. Do not just drop them a message and expect them to act according to your schedule.

> *Advice: involve your client in the tender process.*

Make your client part of your tender process. Seek every option to interact, preferably by phone. You can indicate your tender process and inform the client about your internal qualification process. It is necessary that your client understands you take their project seriously.

If the tender allows you to ask for clarifications, always use this opportunity. All communication with your client is worth the effort. You can use every occasion to influence your client.

> *Advice: keep qualifying during the tender process.*

After the initial qualification of the opportunity, you decide to put the effort into the opportunity. You are trying to win the contract. However, during the tender, the project gets shaped, and you might face additional challenges that might not have been noticed during the initial qualification. These challenges might result in disqualification at a later stage.

The entire team should understand that there is an option to disqualify until the contract is signed. Of course, the more you progress the more difficult it will be to decline, but it always remains an option.

How to Benefit from the Tender Process During Qualification

Often, the tender process is firm, and deadlines are tight. When you are still qualifying the opportunity, the client may already request a list of clarifications. Luckily, most commercial processes are a little flexible and already take into consideration that one of the suppliers may request more time.

In the bridge construction project, the opportunity was qualified, and the first round of clarifications was submitted in time. The client received several clarification sheets from the different suppliers and tried to answer all of the questions. They found out that more time was needed to respond to the clarifications. So, they extended the tender deadline.

During this period, the sales rep worked on risks that were identified in the initial qualification meeting. He used the time wisely and was able to address many of the concerns in the draft bid submission. The draft submission was distributed internally for review four days before the tender deadline.

On the day that the draft was distributed internally, the client notified that one of the suppliers had requested an extension of the tender deadline again. The sales rep decided to keep this information to himself to keep the pressure on his colleagues. One day before the previous submission date, a proposal review meeting was scheduled to give a final "go ahead" for the project. The review meeting resulted in some last improvements, which the sales rep processed in the days before the deadline.

Action: create a tender workflow.

The steps a sales rep needs to take when receiving a tender are similar every time. The glooming deadlines require fast action, which allows all stakeholders sufficient time to prepare and evaluate the tender. The workflow should be triggered when the request from the client is received.

The workflow should start by dividing the different documents into packages relevant to each discipline. The terms and conditions and insurance requirements, including the scope of work, should be forwarded to legal, the scope of work and technical data should be sent to the technical manager, and the QHSE documentation and the scope of work should be sent to the QHSE department. All these packages are to be accompanied by a summary of the project.

The workflow should initiate the start of the bid preparation. Some documents can already be generated, such as financial statements, standard documents (ABC policy, company certificates, track record, etc.).

The workflow should also include an action to go through all tender documents in more detail. This exercise results in a list of attention points, which will be processed further in the workflow and be divided by discipline. Technical concerns will be addressed together with the technical manager, planning concerns with the operations team, and so on.

The workflow should have pre-set milestones, such as initial qualification, clarification submission, draft proposal review, and final qualification. Every loop of activities should come together at milestones.

After each milestone, different flows can be created for different disciplines.

Action: inform your client when the opportunity is qualified by your organization.

Suppliers feel that clients have full control over the process. However, this is not always the case. Clients require the market to propose a solution to a current need. When they issue a request for services, they are not sure that there will be a supplier interested in providing the service. Their system will require more than one supplier to make a good comparison. Most of the time, clients know what to expect from the market, but in times of scarcity, clients cannot be sure that they will get the response they desire.

To provide clients with ease of mind, involve them in your internal processes. You acknowledge receipt of the tender and your willingness to participate. But clients know that a lot can happen after the first few days in the tender process. It is a good habit to inform that client when you take internal decisions to continue with the tender. The clients will appreciate this type of information, so they are surer that they will get the bids they need.

How Does the Tender Pressure fit Into the Qualification Process?

Although it seems that the qualification process is subordinate to the tender process, the tender process has a great impact on the qualification process. There might be risks in the tender process that influence the qualification decision. Often the tender deadlines put pressure on the supplier's tender team. These pressures should not result in taking shortcuts. A review of the tender is required to identify risks. If there is not sufficient time to perform a basic review, it will result in insecurity during the rest of the commercial process.

The tender process also indicates what disciplines have to be involved at what stage. Some tender processes do not initially require a legal review. Clients are confident that there will be a settlement on contractual terms, as long as a good technical solution is created. In that case, the tender process will make qualification easier because the supplier can remain in control a bit longer.

There are more factors resulting from tender pressures. Often, the client requirements cannot be fulfilled by only your company. You will need partners and subcontractors to execute the complete project. The influence that these partners have on the qualification process is significant and is the subject of the next section.

5.2 Supply Chain Pressures

The nicest opportunities, the ones that get you to the next level, require partners. In a lot of cases you need a partner in the commercial process because you miss vital competencies or track records for a significant part of the scope of work. In other cases, you need to create firm agreements to make sure that you can deliver what you promised. This is the case when subcontracted resources are scarce.

The partnerships within your supply chain will put pressure on your qualification process.

Once, I was leading a tender team bidding for a preparation campaign for a large removal scope. An offshore platform needed to be decommissioned with a heavy-lift vessel and we would be the perfect fit for preparing the platform for its final lift. We would cut the legs, remove structural components, attach rigging, secure pipe sections, etc. A big part of the scope involved high-spec welding, which we were unable to do.

For the welding scope, we introduced our partner to the tender process. We agreed on exclusivity to get the full support of the welding company during the tender phase. If we won the project, the welding company would also win the project.

So, now it was not only my colleagues who were putting effort into the tender, it was also a complete team at the welding subcontractor. The expectations from our subcontractor were based on the commercial perspective, which I presented.

Because of the tight deadlines of the project and the amount of work, the welding subcontractor was already on board before we completed the initial qualification. They were a big part of the qualification decision. Without a dedicated subcontractor for the welding scope, we could not have accepted this tender in the first place. We were forced to get the welding subcontractor on the team at a very early stage.

At initial qualification, the project still sounded reasonable. The risks involved were manageable and the complete scope could be covered. Besides that, the potential reward was great. It would provide a significant revenue stream for the next two years and it would secure our place in the market.

The welding subcontractor was not aware of this initial qualification milestone that we passed internally and continued the tender preparations.

My colleagues also continued investigating the project particulars and evaluating its technical and operational impact. The project was shaping up. The first schedules were created, and the full project became visible. The project size estimated at initial qualification was doubled by now and there was still large schedule insecurity. The planning and its insecurity were changing the whole risk profile of the tender.

The welding contractor was not aware of these changing qualification starting points. The welding activities were no longer on the critical path of the project. They were pushing their team to meet the tender deadlines.

A few days before the tender submission deadline, my team had the last review meeting. The final schedules and cost estimates were presented. The profit margins seemed in order but did not match the risk profile. Either the schedules should provide for more contingencies or the cost should be recalculated. The required risk margin was discussed, ranging from 10 to 35%. We continued the discussions. With those risk margins, we needed to ask ourselves if this was the kind of project we should pursue. It would fill our pipeline for 50% of the next two years and it would consume a large part of our resources. If things became out of hand, we would immediately get into a loss situation and far worse consequences for the business could also have possibly resulted.

If we declined, all our work—and the work of the welding subcontractor—would have been for nothing. We felt the pressure of the subcontractors' expectations. We had no idea what to do. If we declined, our relationship with our partner would be seriously affected. Next time, they would not be willing to support us. Declining at this point will not remain unnoticed within the industry and would have a negative impact on our image. The qualification process was overshadowed by the pressures resulting from our cooperation with the subcontractor.

> *Advice: make your supply chain part of your tender journey.*

We should be very open to sharing information with subcontractors. We forward all tender details at an early stage so our partners can be well prepared and that they cannot claim that they missed valuable information. We provide them with the tender deadlines and the terms and conditions that we receive. There are no secrets in the project.

Internally, we often forget the parallel processes going on. Nevertheless, these have a significant impact on our partners' work. We frequently try to keep external factors away from the qualification process by not sharing our internal struggles. We are conditioned to keep internal struggles to ourselves because we feel it is a sign of weakness. Internal struggles are, above all, something you should solve within the doors of your own company.

In the previous tender example, the qualification process backfired on the partner. The partner had no idea about what was going on behind our closed doors. We should have been open about our internal process. We should have provided some insights into qualification milestones, review meetings, and risk identification meetings. These meetings and milestones became a blocking point, and our partners deserved to understand and be involved.

How to Benefit from Supply Chain Pressures in the Qualification Process

Your supply chain has different competencies, equipment, and qualifications. Their companies are formed through different experiences. Their knowledge and skills are why you need them in the project and are the reason for the partnership. You complement each other on the service portfolio, but probably on a wider spectrum as well.

Action: invite your supply chain to review and qualification sessions.

Typically, you hold review and qualification sessions internally. You want to keep communication informal and encourage people to talk freely. Nowadays, this approach might not be a benefit to you anymore. Partnerships between companies are recognized as necessary to battle economic forces. We have to work closely together to maximize the output.

You should consider inviting senior people from within your supplier's organization to your qualification and review sessions. During those sessions, the major project risks are often identified. Frequently, risks are perceived because of a lack of experience. Your partners might not perceive the risks that you foresee and might take over the risk or you can mitigate them as a team. You can only create this environment by inviting partners to the internal sessions.

Action: explain in your tender how the supply chain is formed around the project risks.

The tender requires you to indicate what supply chain partners are required for what parts of the scope. For the critical components of the scope, the client wants to have a really clear understanding of the division of responsibilities. If it is not prescribed in the tender, you will probably want to show it anyway to give your proposal more body.

As a similar exercise of providing clarity of the division-of-scope responsibilities, you could also address the division about project risks. Within the complete partnership structure of your bid submission, you will have assigned all the project's risks. Some risk items are shared among all partners, others are solely in one partner's scope. By notifying your client about the division of risks, the client will gain trust in your bid submission.

By addressing the division of risks, you are forced to put the risks on paper. All tender partners understand each other's risks and then can relate better to the questions and concerns that are raised by a particular partner.

How the Supply Chain Pressures Fit into the Qualification Process

A bike is a metaphor I like to use for tender partnerships. The main contractor forms the frame, but the frame cannot ride without wheels, a handlebar, pedals, and brakes. Some items can be easily replaced, others have a significant stake. If a wheel is missing, riding the bike will be impossible. It is really important that the wheels and the frame can rely on each other. With a frame and wheels, you can move forward.

If the handlebar, pedals, brakes, or saddle are missing, you can get them replaced. For wheels or the frame, that is different.

When the main contractor decides to disqualify, the wheels will remain jobless. They are an integral part of the complete package. They cannot jump to the next main contractor since the wheel will not fit that frame.

When you decide to start building a bike together, it is hard for one of the components to just choose not to contribute anymore. There is real pressure from the system to keep creating the full package and to market a complete bicycle. We should not underestimate this kind of pressure on the qualification process. It is necessary to establish open communication lines within tender partnerships.

The supply chain, therefore, has a big influence on the tender submission. Another real pressure resulting from the tender pressure is formed by the specifications, including the applicable legal terms. Those are subjects of the next section.

5.3 Specs Pressures

Liza and Richard have no idea that their paths will cross in the near future. They have apparently completely different destinations but are trying to meet in the middle. If you plotted their journey on the X-Model, which was designed to show how people use their skills and qualifications to improve productivity, Liza's journey would lead through more sales and Richard's journey to a fulfilled project with no risk. The X-Model was designed to describe individual or organizational success through employee engagement but could just as well serve to find the sweet spot in the buyer-seller dance.

When Liza gets to work, she is full of energy. She is determined to find new opportunities for the software company she is working for. Her goal is to sell their services on favorable terms. She is not going for quick sales but regards a sale as being good when she is able to win the project for the terms that are determined by her company.

When Richard arrives at his desk, he is determined to avoid risks as much as possible. He does not only want to procure a software package, but he also wants the supplier take responsibility of all the risks involved. When Richard signs a purchase order, he wants to have his terms reflected on it.

Liza and Richard have met before. Liza presented her software package and convinced many stakeholders at Richard's organization. Richard liked Liza's story too and included Liza's business on the supplier shortlist, together with four other companies.

Richard gathered all functional requirements from his colleagues. He added standard terms and conditions, qualification requirements, and a pricing template. Before sending the package, he directed his legal team to draw up a set of specific terms and conditions, which form an add-on to the standard ones.

Richard uploaded the completed tender into their sourcing system. He entered the shortlisted companies and hit the 'submit' button. Moments later, Liza received a notification from the sourcing system that a new ITT event had been issued for her attention. Liza tried to log onto the system that she had used before. After having to change her password, she started working her way into the system.

First, there were numerous qualification questions, which she filled in on auto-pilot hoping to get to the part where she could download Richard's tender package. Liza was almost discouraged when she got the message that she had passed the qualification tab. She noticed that the combined tender package was 8 MB and she wondered how her clients always managed to create these immense packages. Maybe her client's procurement team would be paid by the MB?

> *Advice: don't get demotivated when presented with bureaucracy.*

Once Liza opened the sourcing system, she already found herself looking at the clock. She had 45 minutes until her next meeting started. She hoped she could get to the essence of the tender before that time, so she could prepare to distribute it internally after her meeting.

She had completed many tender processes in the past. She enjoys working on the perfect solution but disliked the administrative burden. Liza had the feeling that she could spend her time better than by filling in standard forms, but she had learned to overcome her negative beliefs and tried to see it as another challenge on the road to the contract.

> *Advice: focus on the showstoppers.*

Often, major obstacles pop up in tender documents. You know that some of your colleagues will respond intensely to these challenges. You can choose to hide these points or to make them appear more attractive, but in the end, they might cause a dead end. Always be prepared to address them at the beginning of the process.

The potential showstoppers should be discussed with the client. Your client might not be aware of the impact of these points or might pretend they were not aware when including them in the requirements. They are often hidden in the scope of work and only referenced once. Try to identify them and address them immediately.

> *Advice: use clarification rounds to discuss specifications.*

Every invitation to bid for a project includes the opportunity to ask questions. The art of asking the right questions is underestimated in tender processes. Every commercial process offers different ways to ask questions. There might be clarification meetings, formal tender clarification forms, or the client might leave communication lines open for discussion among many. Always use the available clarification option.

The clarification process can add to the creation of a better relationship with your client and you can use it to prepare the client for what they will be receiving at the bid due date.

Don't be afraid to ask many questions. You should think about how you ask for clarification. Try to ask open questions and explain the reason for asking the question.

If you are obliged to use standard forms to request clarification, be prepared that your competition will see your questions and the client's answers as well. Your competition will understand what your focus service offerings will be. Don't be discouraged by the fact that your competitor is getting an insight into your attempts to win the project.

When you have found potential showstoppers in the tender, do not ask if this showstopper can be eliminated. It is better to ask the reason the client included that particular item and explain why you are wondering. The client will answer those questions honestly and might even consider limiting the effect of the showstopper. You did not ask to eliminate it, but you made the topic discussable.

> *Advice: sales should offer colored glasses to their organizations.*

Requests for quotations often appear to be black and white. There seems to be no middle way. This can cause your colleagues to protest. It is sales that should provide a positive view on the requirements. Sales should be able to explain why certain things ended up in the RFQ, how they can be mitigated, and put them into perspective.

The sales team is not only there to sell the service to the client, but they are also there to sell it internally. Sales should make the operational teams enthusiastic about the new opportunity. Potential blocking points should be addressed appropriately and mitigated.

> *Advice: try to influence the specifications before the RFQ is sent out.*

We all know that the better the specifications meet our unique competencies the greater the chances of success. All selling methods and theories (SPIN, Challenger Sale, etc.) refer to this in some form. We should try to be in discussion with our clients before the requirements are fixed. We should attempt to advise our clients and manipulate the specifications in our favor along the way.

During the qualification process, you will find it easier to qualify opportunities that fit your unique competencies. You will have less trouble getting your organization enthusiastic and you can prepare your proposal more effectively.

How to Benefit From the Tender Specifications

The jungle of specifications is dense. They are unique to your industry and are part of the industry's playing rules. Navigating your way through the specifications is a daunting exercise, but inevitable during the qualification process. Seemingly small items in the specifications can potentially alter the course of your tender process and affect your chances of winning the contract.

You need to understand how to work your way through the specifications and how to benefit from them. You can regard the specifications as being a starting point to further advise your client or to create a win-win negotiation strategy.

Action: create a tender evaluation form.

Once you receive a tender, you will feel overwhelmed by the amount of information in it. To get clarity for yourself and your colleagues, you should adopt a tender evaluation form. The form includes a section on the scope of work, the clients involved, your initial thoughts on the supply chain requirements, and the planning. You should go into more detail addressing the three or four main contractual risks you typically find in tender packages. This makes them visible immediately.

An evaluation form will help you and your colleagues throughout the tender process. The information entered into the form can be used on several occasions through it.

In the case of smaller RFQs, you can choose to limit it to a few points, but making the process generic also makes it more recognizable.

Action: communicate clearly about showstoppers.

Experiences from the past, or current developments, introduce real showstoppers. These showstoppers are parts of the tender, which you cannot accept under any circumstance. Examples that I stumbled across are incorrect governing laws, uncapped liability, or signs of bribery.

In recent years, organizations are becoming more and more concerned about other aspects of international business. These organizations create awareness of human rights or the environment. They are committing themselves to sustainable development goals, which have an impact on the qualification process. Some organizations refuse to work in countries that promote gender inequality, are harmful to the environment, or are in other conflict with their belief system.

When receiving a tender, be truly committed to your showstoppers and communicate them directly to your prospect or client. If you are straight from the beginning, you might work on solving the issue together or clearing the path for cooperation.

Action: use price to negotiate specifications.

Specifications are often not carved in stone. Be prepared to discuss the specifications and highlight where the bottlenecks are. You will soon find out what specifications are important to your client and which ones are nice-to-haves. Use this knowledge to your advantage when negotiating.

Typically, your client wants to bring your price down. Be aware that you can use the specifications, especially legal specifications, to maintain your profit margin. The risks you have in a project are different than the risks for your client. It is the salesperson's responsibility to find the added value and keep the required price levels.

How the Specifications Fit into the Qualification Process

The specifications have a direct impact on the commercial outcome. Unfavorable tender conditions will result in a lower chance of winning. When the specifications are in line with your company's competencies, you will have more chance of winning and your commercial process will be smoother. During the qualification process, you estimate the win chances, which makes the specifications a significant part of the qualification process.

The specifications will have a direct impact on the project fit. In the next paragraphs, we will take a look at the overall fit of the project in relation to your company.

5.4 Project Fit

It's Sunday night and your spouse asked you to cook her favorite dish. It is the one that your mother taught you and that you have been cooking since second grade. You can prep the meal with your eyes closed. And, best of all, you know your spouse will love it!!

This is the same feeling that you sometimes have when a request from your client drops in your mailbox and it exactly meets your core competency. You almost forget that it is sitting in your mailbox because you know you can prepare the bid overnight. You don't even worry about the deadline since you know that you can process the request within hours.

The perfect project fits right into the expertise and experience of your company. You do not need to worry about qualification. You know that the opportunity is qualified. The only qualification hurdle is resource planning. But you know that this project is so easy that everyone will feel comfortable expanding the resources (temporarily).

> *Advice: cherish these perfect projects like your children.*

Since these projects are so normal for you, you might forget their importance. It is these projects where your organization can execute without project risk while keeping a good margin. You might feel really confident about the outcome of the tender process, but you still have to give it the attention it deserves.

> *Advice: get a good mix of project fits.*

You should build your business on the projects that have the perfect fit. You can create a solid business on these projects. But your business will need to develop broader. There is always a risk that the competition will do better on your core competency, so you have to build competencies outside your initial offering. You can only build new competencies when your prospects give you the chance to learn.

You can use the perfect-fit project as a step up and gain the trust of your existing customers. When your current client base is happy with your performance, they will invite you to add value to other challenges they have. You should accept some of these opportunities although they are not a perfect fit. The other qualification criteria will guide you in the selection of the right opportunities.

How to Benefit From the Perfect-Fit Project

When you do not need to spend a lot of energy to get the perfect opportunity across the line internally and you can win the project with the same ease, you can use your surplus energy to increase your business or get home early.

Action: use the perfect-fit projects to upsell.

The easy projects will get you at the table with your prospect. You will get the chance to offer additional services. You can use the opportunity to combine the perfect-fit project with additional services as one inquiry. In that way, you might take over the scope of your competitor because you have better chances with the scope of your perfect fit.

The qualification process for the upsell as part of the tender will be more difficult. You might need to convince your colleagues, but it is worth growing the business with this account and maximizing the result.

Action: get your junior salesperson involved in the perfect-fit projects.

Everybody within your organization understands the perfect-fit opportunities. Everyone can support the new person on the team. Junior salespeople can practice their sales skills and find their way within your organization. It is relatively easy to get results soon after starting the job. They will gain confidence along the way.

Assign a peer to safeguard the quality of the sales process. In light of cherishing the opportunities like your children, you would also not let a ten-year-old babysit your children. You should be very cautious with easy projects since they remain important to your business.

How Does the Project fit in the Qualification Process?

The ideal project provides a shortcut in the qualification process. When your spouse asked you to prepare her favorite meal, you knew you could not refuse. You did not start a discussion on why you should do the cooking, or how to prepare it. You know what to do and you can complete the task with one hand behind your back.

The perfect project provides you with a foundation for your current business and for growing the business. You will have energy left to devote to diversifying and upselling. You will not leave opportunities on the table because of slow internal processes. You can immediately jump into the selling process.

Since everyone within the organization can prepare the commercial proposal and everyone in the operational departments knows how to execute the project, there seems to be very little reason for disqualification.

The fit of the project within the current core competencies forms a starting point for the qualification process. When there is no risk involved and the resources are available the majority of the qualification process can be dismissed.

It is almost too boring to perform sales on this project. On the other hand, it provides a lot of opportunities to add additional value to your clients. And there is always a risk of the competition taking over these kinds of projects.

Together with the tender specifications and supply chain pressures, the project fit determines the complexity of the tender process. If the outcome of the tender pressures is difficult, you will need the other pressures described in this book to complete a firm qualification decision.

5.5 Summary

Selling is arguably the toughest job in the world, but one that provides a sense of victory when you move a step closer to winning your next project. You have put all your energy in to find your lead, get in front of him or her, communicate until you get to a point when the tender or request for quotation is dropped in your mailbox.

That is the point when the real challenge starts. You are always focused on getting external attention. You begin to build relationships outside the walls of your company. You have the feeling that you are a lonely knight sent beyond to fight a commercial battle. When you return to your castle with a victory in clear sight, you feel as though you have entered a different world.

When you were talking to your prospect, you provided an honest overview of your company's competencies. But you tried to focus on the positive issues. You forgot about the fact that bureaucracy is an internal hurdle you need to jump over to land the contract internally. You 'forget' to explain how hard it is to buy from you.

You have used the tactic of scarcity to create a sense of urgency with your client. Now, when the client has acted, you have to use the same aspect of scarcity to involve the prospect in your internal qualification process. These are hard processes and potential clients can only appreciate the process if you communicate clearly and professionally.

In this chapter, we defined some of the key pressures that result directly from the tender. The tender process is defined by the contents of the tender package provided by the prospect. Lengthy and complex tender processes create a burden in the qualification process. If the tender requires a lot of resources, the opportunity might be disqualified because of the lack of those resources.

Then there is a blend of specifications present in the tender package. The technical scope of work makes the project fit, or not. All the other specifications, such as terms and conditions, insurance requirements, HSE requirements, and other administrative duties do not make the tender that sexy. Salespeople try to neglect these exercises, but the process will require them to act on these additional specifications. They are just part of today's business.

The qualification decision cannot be capped by a standard framework. This will kill any entrepreneurial spirit and will leave limited room for creativity. By accepting that there are exceptions, you will be making a better qualification decision.

My unique qualification process

1.
2.
3.
4
5.
6.

Implementation

You have been made aware of the many factors influencing the qualification process. You might be a little overwhelmed at this point, but still feel you need to do something with all the information you have learned. In this chapter, I will help you to make sense of all the factors influencing your qualification process.

First, we will dive into the building blocks that will form your future process. After that, I will provide my unique qualification process that I used during my time as manager of a sales team in the oil and gas industry. Lastly, some starting points will be provided to outline your own process.

If you have reached this point in the book, it means that you are willing to improve. You might want to get clarity on your own process or to give clarity to your sales team. A written qualification process has a few advantages:

- It puts your insecurities to rest.
- The rest of the organization understands your reasoning.
- It can be used to train new colleagues.
- It provides room to deviate.
- It requires everyone to overthink the qualification decision.

When you have outlined your qualification process, you can make the right decisions. When you log the factors that made you come to a qualification conclusion, you can revisit them when a project is completed. The feedback can be incorporated into a revised process. You will learn as a team by trying to perfect the process.

The process is vague until you start to narrow it down. Cutting it into small chunks makes the process digestible. We call the chunks, building blocks.

Building Blocks
The qualification building blocks are not used to construct a wall for doing business. They provide a starting point to identify what can be done. The building blocks actually provide an opening for qualification. They are therefore building blocks and not blocking blocks.

Many qualification processes seem to be designed for the opposite. They are designed by the organization to put sales on a tight leash. The argument is that sales should target in a laser-sharp manner. In real life, this is not how things work. If the systems are too rigid, sales will find a work around. The sales team should take the lead in creating the qualification process and go beyond the standard framework and the established service portfolio.

Who Brings the Opportunities?
When my Dream Client called me in Chapter 2, I knew I had to go the extra mile. I knew that qualification would be hard based on appetite, personal timing, and project execution. It was Frank who called me just before Christmas with a challenging technical problem he was facing. He was employed by one of my Dream Clients and he had an urgent need. Those two factors made the opportunity qualified. I used my personal timing and personal excitement to get this project qualified.

Growing your business can mean diversifying your client portfolio with clients in different industries. For the growth to happen, you will need Future A clients. Once a predefined Future A client knocks on your door, you have to broaden your qualification perspective. A narrow approach to qualification will not get you the new customer. You should use the company's ambition, project potential, and supply chain pressures to counterbalance the difficult specifications and the lack of project fit.

After onboarding your new agent in a remote country, you will need to give him some slack. You want to motivate him to bring in good opportunities. You cannot expect him to find the nicest opportunity immediately. You will need to create a supportive environment. He might bring a project that is not an immediate fit, with a too-short lead time, and with an incomplete standard framework (BANT). You need the opportunity to pass the qualification test to educate and motivate the new agent.

When the new person or agent on the team brings in an opportunity with a Dream Client or a Future A client, the qualification process should be relaxed a little further. You want to motivate the team to win the project. You want to use the opportunity, not only to educate the newbie, but also to secure the new business. The qualification process should not be an obstruction.

6.1 Building Blocks

Urgent requests from clients provide a fertile base for margin. When a prospect or client is experiencing pain, they are comfortable spending a premium to solve their need on short notice. The appetite of your company and the project potential should allow you to dive into the opportunity with opportunism and a sense of reality. Additionally, you should not let your personal timing stand in the way. If the opportunity drops in at an inconvenient time, you have the obligation to get your team involved.

When you are faced with a drying pipeline, you have to be creative in filling it. You still need to qualify hard, but you have to gather tools to get less favorable opportunities qualified. You can match the opportunity with the company's ambition in a creative manner. Or you can point the qualification commission to the indirect potential of the project. It requires creativity from the salesperson.

The opposite is true as well. When you are nearing a deadline or a holiday, and you cannot take on another opportunity, you should act accordingly by addressing this issue within your sales team and your company. Opportunities should not get lost because they interfere with the planning of one individual.

6.2 My Unique Qualification Process

It is not my intention to make you adopt my qualification process. The process is unique for every company, and you can tweak in a way that is unique to your business. Nevertheless, my qualification process can get you started. Certain parts are relatively universal.

The qualification process I describe in this section is the one I used during my time at a small company in the oil and gas industry. My team and I sold special lifting projects to all major oil and gas operators all over the world. Usually, my qualification process starts when an opportunity is presented to me.

I teach my team not to disqualify before talking to me, their peers, or operational colleagues. Even when the opportunity does not pass the qualification bar, I try to let the client conclude we are not the right supplier.

In the next section, I will describe the different steps of my qualification process.

My Qualification Process Steps

The opportunity is presented by different channels, which often have a different start to the qualification process. The opportunity can be presented by a team member, a project manager who is working on another project with the client; it can be dropped in one of our mailboxes; or it can be presented by a formal tender. The qualification process, however, follows the same path.

Step 1: For which end client is the project?

One of the decisive factors of qualification is the end client. There might be a party in between, e.g., main contractor, but the end client is the focus at this stage.

I evaluate in what category the end client falls. I identify four categories: existing client, former client, Dream client / Future A, or general prospect.

Existing clients know what our company is capable of providing. When they present a project, it is most likely qualified. We will be focusing on retaining the business with this existing client. We try to use the lessons learned in the past to improve our offer and our service. Since these clients offer a solid foundation for business continuity, we are likely to qualify the opportunity, even when the project is not a perfect fit or the timeline is too short.

Former clients often request quotations to benchmark to our competition. We will qualify harder to make sure that we stand a chance in the competition.

If the end client pops up on the list of Dream Clients or Future A Clients, we qualify based on the project fit and project execution. If the timeline of the project allows for superior project execution, we will qualify Future A clients to make sure that we are on their radar.

General prospects are those that do not turn up on any of the lists. They have not bought our services before and are not part of our target lists. They provide us with opportunities based on our marketing efforts. The inquiry is often not a perfect fit. The prospect put effort into making the tender as generic as possible to ensure enough suppliers offer a quote. For these opportunities, we will strictly qualify.

Step 2: How is the opportunity brought to us?

The way the opportunity found its way to my desk indicates the level of seriousness. When the opportunity is preceded by many sales activities, and a relationship has already been created, the opportunity is more likely to fit our competencies. The responsible salesperson has put in a lot of effort to get this opportunity, which explains his or her behavior during the qualification process.

When an inquiry is sent to a company mailbox without much interaction, the opportunity is more likely to be disqualified. We had no influence on structuring the project, the requested project execution does not fit our way of working, and the salesperson is not overly motivated to win the project. These opportunities are often presented by general prospects and are generally heading toward disqualification.

The more history there is before the opportunity is presented, the more likely the opportunity will be qualified.

Step 3: How do we use the traditional qualification framework?

We chose to use the BANT qualification method. This is a simple way to analyze the relationship with the client and with the decision-making unit. We chose this method because of its simplicity. There is no need to overcomplicate the process. We rely on the quality of the sales individuals.

We structure our conversations based on the BANT criteria (budget, authority, needs, and timeline). We ask ourselves to what levels we could get the required confidence on those factors. If one of the criteria is lacking, we will further investigate it. When one criterion is missing entirely, we are likely to disqualify.

The previous question of how the opportunity was presented is closely connected to the framework. When there is a long history before the opportunity comes up, it is obvious that the BANT criteria are better.

Step 4: What is the current mood of our company?

Sometimes, the perfect project comes at totally the wrong time. It might be that there are organizational circumstances that influence the appetite. In other times in the business's life, the motivation to win the contract may be missing. This factor should not influence the qualification process. However, when there are hiccups identified, it is better to address them during the qualification process.

When the current mood is not supportive in any way of the presented opportunity, we would disqualify after internal consultation. We would always discuss this with company management to check our assumptions.

Step 5: Are the scope of work and specifications in line with what and how we offer?

The opportunity is never a perfect fit. Even when you have the chance to structure the potential project and the tender documents, there will always be aspects that are not working for you. Additional scope is added for which you need to subcontract. There might be terms and conditions that are showstoppers. Or you cannot commit to the requested lead times. When the project scope or the specs are too far off your offering, there might be a reason to disqualify.

The other factors, e.g., type of end client or your ability to influence the presented opportunity through clarification rounds, will influence the level of opportunity acceptance. The projects of end clients who are on one of your lists (existing client, Dream client, Future A) are more likely to be qualified even if the scope of work or specifications provide a lot of challenges. For certain clients, you simply go the extra mile.

Step 6: Are there any commitments to other stakeholders?

Supply chain partners or new agents might require you to participate in tender processes because you have a mutual commitment. You can try to convince them of the reason for disqualification, but you cannot do that too often. You want to keep the relationship working and sometimes you need to invest by qualifying not-so-interesting opportunities.

The same is true for the occasion when you have a new salesperson on your team. You might want to qualify an opportunity for the sake of training or to keep the new hire motivated.

Step 7: Who should work on the opportunity?

The salesperson assigned to an opportunity can make all the difference. Qualified opportunities should be assigned to a motivated salesperson. If for some reason the opportunity cannot be reassigned, e.g., no interest from sales colleagues or the salesperson is protective of his or her opportunities, then you might need to disqualify. There is no need to try to win a contract with an unmotivated salesforce.

Process Outcome

The whole reason for the qualification exercise is to focus on the right opportunities. All factors play a role in making the right qualification decision. The process outcome is a go/no-go type of decision. A no-go means that the opportunity is disqualified and that the prospect needs to find another supplier for their project.

A go will mean that you will provide the client with a solution for the challenge. The outcome of the qualification process is never a simple go. There are many lessons taken and risks identified during the qualification process. All these additional outputs will offer room to improve the final offer.

Besides the topics addressed during the qualification process, the salesperson will keep working on the relationship with the client. It is the responsibility of the salesperson to get a clear picture of the commercial playing field. The presented opportunity is not the real challenge or may be just a part of the problem. The qualification process can help fill in the blanks. It provides the salesperson with tools and reasons to keep reaching out to the potential client.

So, the qualification process is not only there to make a go/no-go decision. It is also there to optimize your offer and to maximize the winning ratio.

Conclusion

I have outlined my general qualification process. The process is not a rigid flow of decisions, but it supports good decision making. These decisions are not only rational. There are many subjective factors influencing the qualification process. By considering both rational and subjective factors, you can come to a well-formed conclusion.

We have seen how my qualification process works. I try to involve the client as much as possible in this process, not only to get the required input but also to improve our business relationship with the client. How we should involve our clients during the qualification process is the subject of the next section.

6.3 Involve Your Client

The scope of this book is not to teach you how to sell. It is to explain how to get rich by focusing on the right opportunities at the right time. It is about qualification. Nevertheless, there is a great deal of client interaction involved. The outcome of the qualification process immediately affects your relationship with the client.

You will need to involve your client in the qualification process. The process is not solely an internal matter. Just as much as you need to qualify with your client, it is the client who needs to be qualified by your organization. Everyone understands that we cannot offer value on all projects all the time. We live in a world in which resources are scarce, so all parties in the commercial process need to understand the things they can expect from each other.

Traditional qualification frameworks solely focus on the client and their decision-making unit. They make sure that we understand all criteria relevant to making a good sale, but there are many more factors influencing the qualification process.

In this section, I will outline how you can communicate with your client during the qualification process. Communication during the qualification process adds to the depth of the relationship between you and your client. Make the client part of your journey and you will better understand each other's reasoning. You need to create acceptance at every stage.

Opportunity Acceptance

The speed of your first steps will significantly increase your chances of success. Your client will require at least three quotations to make sure that one fits their needs. They will try to get five parties to accept the opportunity since they know that two might withdraw during the tender process. The faster your client feels that they will get their three quotes, the sooner they stop their quest to invite more companies to join the tender process.

I created a habit of immediately responding to new requests. I confirm acceptance of the opportunity and explain when I will evaluate the information and revert.

> *"Thanks for your interest in our company and services. We have received your request in good order and will respond as soon as possible.*
>
> *Since we have done business before, I assume that we can add value. In that case, you will receive an offer before your deadline. But please allow me until Wednesday morning at 10:00 AM to evaluate your requirements."*

After this step, I dive into the process defined in the previous chapter. Once the project seems to fit our capabilities and is with a promising client, I will involve an operational colleague to check internal capacity during the requested execution period.

Before the deadline set in my confirmation email, I respond to the client with a confirmation of opportunity acceptance, or I will decline.

> *"After evaluating your requirements, I concluded that we can add value to your project. We will prepare a solid quotation before your deadline.*
>
> *There are some concerns, which I would like to discuss with you over a phone call. Some of these concerns are:*
>
> *Concern 1*
>
> *Concern 2*
>
> *….*
>
> *Are you available to run through the project with me tomorrow afternoon?"*

The concerns mentioned in the email are real concerns. They often relate to the execution schedule, additional scope, or some technical concerns. By outlining the concerns, you establish a foundation of trust. You create an open communication environment. It will allow you to get on a phone call to work your way into the opportunity.

Communication on the Qualification Process

Your client is not doing business with you. He is doing business with your entire company. He understands that you are part of a complex structure and that you cannot act autonomously. It is your responsibility to qualify the opportunity, but you can use your leverage to involve your client (a little bit) in your internal process.

During the first call with your client in which you discussed some initial concerns, you touched upon the process of creating a commercial and technical proposal. You should summarize your discussion in an email, so both you and your client are on the same page. In this email, you can involve your client in the process.

The main advantage of having an open line of communication is that you can call the client whenever you face a roadblock or objections. At the same time, your client has the feeling you are taking his project seriously. You are building rapport with your client.

> *"Thanks for today's conversation. We have addressed my initial concerns.*
>
> *Resolution concern 1*
>
> *Conclusion concern 2*
>
> *....*
>
> *I will involve engineering and project management to prepare a solid proposal. They will have questions which I would like to raise with you. I expect to have these questions before the end of next week.*
>
> *If there are any showstoppers presented by my colleagues, I will immediately involve you. If things change on your end, please let me know as well."*

With every step try to create awareness of the next part of the process, especially when you require the client to do something, prepare him to do so. Always invite your client to call you as well during the process.

Once your qualification process is complete, make sure to confirm that with the client. If you have certain doubts or need information, communicate this to your client and note if the responses will affect whether or not you will be quoting, or if they will have an impact on the commercial proposal.

> *"We had internal discussions, and some queries were raised. We have listed the queries in the attached clarification sheet. It would be great to get your feedback.*
>
> *The answers to these queries will affect the proposal but they are not showstoppers. You can expect a proposal within two weeks, but at least one week after receiving your feedback.*
>
> *I will give you a call tomorrow to find out if all my queries are clear. Perhaps we can address some of them immediately, so we can speed up the process."*

During that call, you will work together with the client. You will provide clarity on the reason for raising certain questions. Often, the client does not understand the relevance of the queries. It is important to get them to understand their importance, so they are more willing to answer.

Proposal Preparation Phase

Once you have collected all the details, it is time to create the best proposal you can. Address your concerns and the client's concerns. Try to benchmark your offer to an alternative solution and provide whatever is needed to optimize your proposal.

The perfect tender is not part of the scope of this book. Nevertheless, I want to give you one more piece of advice.

Three days before the deadline, send your client an unpriced proposal and ask for his feedback. Call him the day after to gather feedback.

The added value of this sneak peek is that you get a final chance to bond with your client. You can find out what red flags your client will be raising. You can still tweak your proposal to improve the outcome. You might even find the chance to talk about pricing.

If your competition has already quoted, you might get a feeling about their offer during this phone call. If the client wants you to win, they might share a little of the proposal from your competition. They will judge your unpriced proposal based on the contents of your competitor's proposal.

Additionally, you will provide assurance to your client that they will receive the quotation they require. Clients will trust you more if you keep them in the loop during the final stage of tendering as well.

Communicate to Win

This section is devoted to the art of selling. It is an incomplete picture of everything you need to do as a salesperson as you work continuously on your relationship with prospects and clients.

In my experience, however, it is the qualification process during which salespersons are hiding. While they are delighted when they receive a request for a quotation, they are on tenterhooks trying to get it qualified. In complex sales environments and solution selling, the salesperson often has the feeling that the hard selling is taking place internally rather than externally. Many objections are thrown at the salesperson from colleagues as to why they should not quote, and this can cause great insecurity about the outcome of the qualification process.

A strategy adopted by salespeople is to fight this struggle on their own. They feel it is a sign of weakness if they need to involve their client in the qualification process.

I emphasize the value of making your clients part of your journey. They will appreciate your vulnerability and understand that you are part of a complex environment, similar to theirs. They are as insecure as you are. Your clients need your competitive quote and are willing to contribute to realizing this shared goal.

I have provided some tools for you to start communicating with your clients during the qualification process. Do not let yourself be limited by the tools I have presented. Creativity will be rewarded. At least make sure you keep talking to your client by keeping communication lines open.

6.4 Summary

Maybe this chapter is the best of the whole book. You started the journey in this book by having a traditional qualification framework. You soon found out that there is a multitude of other factors involved in qualification but now you have transitioned into an aware salesperson.

When starting this last chapter, you might have had the feeling that all of this information was rather overwhelming. This chapter, however, structured your thoughts and showed you that the process is not as complex as it might have seemed. It has transitioned you into a competent person by providing you with the tools to start creating your own qualification process.

The building blocks have been presented to you in the previous chapters of this book. This last chapter showed you how to connect them together to create your unique qualification process. It forces you to consider your qualification process in a more practical way.

During the process, you probably had flashbacks to past experiences since the qualification process is not always pleasant. There might have been occasions when you had to decline an opportunity at a very late stage. You might recall those opportunities well. It is those opportunities in which you suffered some kind of inner pain that has most likely motivated you to perfect your qualification game.

I outlined my basic qualification process. The process is simple to digest and might provide you with a starting point for your own qualification process. I hope that my process inspired you, but that you adjust it to fit your own needs.

The last section has pulled you out of your routine of considering the qualification process as an internal process. I showed you how the qualification process can be used to improve your relationship with your client. By establishing a healthy foundation, you can optimize your success. You can add value to your client during the qualification process by clearly communicating the steps you need to take and which objections and concerns you need to address during the process.

After you have finished reading this book, I am available to support you on your journey. I have created many other materials regarding the qualification process, which I hope you explore.

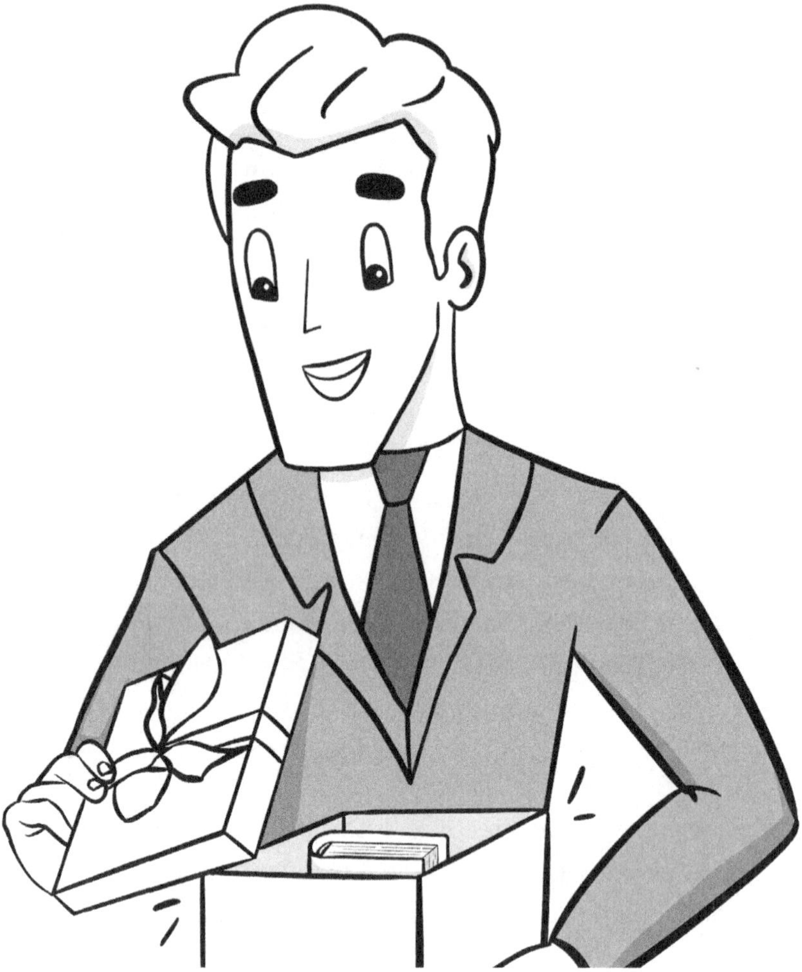

Conclusion – Next Steps

Wow, you made it to the end. You must feel overwhelmed by all the information you have read. I understand this. It took me over a decade to figure this stuff out. It took me more than a year to put it on paper. And I asked you to digest all the factors influencing the qualification process in just six chapters. Instead of feeling overwhelmed, I hope you feel that this is a small gift to you. It is a concise summary of a decade of study at your disposal.

I shared only my findings, the things that are working for me and the people in my communities. You can be confident that you can implement a proven qualification system guided by the steps in this book. It can be a proven add-on to your current system, filling a gap that you may have been experiencing.

You took the first step on your journey to make the qualification process work for you. By now, you might have lost the motivation to implement all of these steps I have advised. This is perfectly normal. There is so much information to digest that you probably don't know where to start.

I want you to revisit the one project you thought of when getting your copy of this book. At the time, you experienced pain or frustration and felt that the qualification process could have made all the difference. You wanted to transform into a razor-sharp sales machine, only spending time on the opportunities that would make you and the people around you rich. You were ready to transform.

It is now time to take the next step. Start implementing the lessons from this book as part of your daily routine. I would recommend you start with the following steps:

- Take five tender processes, which you lost or had to quit before submitting.
- Decide what the reasons were for losing or withdrawing?
- Think about what exceptions you want in your qualification process? Consider: Dream clients, Future A clients, urgency, and other factors described in chapters 2 and 3.
- Describe in five bullet points how you and your organizations can influence the qualification process differently? In other words, if you had an opportunity nine months ago, and a similar opportunity now, what might the issues be that would cause you to qualify differently?
- Present your findings to your sales team and management and get their feedback.

There are no shortcuts. I spent over a year creating this book and optimizing the lessons in it. Nevertheless, I understand it will never replace coaching in real life. I am here to help you to improve your qualification process. I want to transform you from just being aware to becoming fully professional. I want to change your qualification process from a corporate tool to a highly effective sales machine.

I have coached other salespeople through webinars, masterclasses, and in-company. I invite you to connect on my socials to get the support you need at the time you need it. You will be kept in the loop on live events, free webinars, and other great stuff to keep you on your journey.

With all of this said, I want you to enjoy sales again and not be frustrated by focusing on the wrong opportunities. I want you to become a pro in detecting the right opportunities to make you rich financially and in life.

All that is rest for me to do is to thank you for starting this journey and becoming part of my world.

About the Author

The scarcity of the resource of 'time' made Bram van Oirschot write his second book. After his first book, "Industrial Sales – A Roadmap to Increase Your Sales Globally," Bram continues to inspire salespeople and business owners worldwide.

Bram van Oirschot is a commercial professional that writes from within the trenches. He knows exactly what his readers are experiencing because he is amidst the commercial challenges.

Bram is a firm believer in cooperation rather than competition. He believes in sharing knowledge rather than trying to outweigh each other. His friendly, comforting way of writing will please his readers.

Pieces of Advice

Create your Dream Clients list to know when to accelerate. 29

Create internal awareness of your Dream Clients. 30

Tender and execution resources are the main factors when qualifying dream clients. 30

Never disqualify opportunities with Dream Clients. 31

Educate your Dream Client by participating in tenders. 31

Look out for company diversification needs and align with corresponding Future A Clients. 36

When tendering for your Future A, think long term. 37

Only disqualify once with your Future A. 37

1 in 5 Dream Clients should be on your Future A list. 37

Disqualify tenders that require a short tender reaction time. 38

Integrate urgency into your qualification process. 42

Let your client set the budget. 43

Be honest about the possibilities. 43

Be very careful to qualify for urgency with Future A companies. .. 44

Keep the qualification process within the sales team. 48

Use the opportunity qualification process to streamline sales and execution capacity. 48

Identify the level of risk appetite on a quarterly basis. 60

Link the risk appetite to ambition. 61

Journal the issues that have an impact on appetite. 61

Analyze the qualification trends within your company. 62

Identify and communicate the long-term ambition and vision. 67

Streamline corporate goals with the company purpose. 68

Disqualify hard if the opportunity does not fit the
    corporate ambition. 68

Use your pipeline to flatten the resource utilization factors. 74

Provide clarity on your pipeline visually. 75

Find out what the personal preference is of your
    operational colleagues. 76

Work on storytelling to give your opportunity an extra edge. 82

Paint the long-term picture. 82

Show empathy for the situation you put your colleagues into. 83

Search for connections between ambition and project potential. .. 83

Use experience to estimate the total project value. 83

Recognize your mood and that of the people around you. 96

Track holiday planning and mitigate the inappropriate
    disqualification risk. 97

Monitor individual sales pipelines. 97

Use the mental peaks. 98

Discuss opportunities with peers. 103

Recognize the fears within the sales team. 104

Empathy is your best friend. 105

Keep the excitement as long as you can. 110

Use excitement to convince and facts to support. 111

Spread your excitement during the qualification process. 111

Save the first opportunities and qualify at least half. 116

Understand the correlation between disqualification and motivation. 117

Let new people target broadly in the beginning. 117

Always be prepared to escalate. 128

Manage expectations from the start of the qualification process. ... 129

Involve your client in the tender process. 129

Keep qualifying during the tender process. 129

Make your supply chain part of your tender journey. 136

Don't get demotivated when presented with bureaucracy. 141

Focus on the showstoppers. 142

Use clarification rounds to discuss specifications. 142

Sales should offer colored glasses to their organizations. 143

Try to influence the specifications before the RFQ is sent out. 144

Cherish these perfect projects like your children. 148

Get a good mix of project fits. 148

Printed in Great Britain
by Amazon